ALL ABOUT ILYAS

A Story about Raising a Foster Child

APRIL MARTIN

Copyright © 2018 April Martin

ISBN: 978-1-63263-680-5

All rights reserved. No part of this publication may be reproduced, stored in a retrieval system, or transmitted in any form or by any means, electronic, mechanical, recording or otherwise, without the prior written permission of the author.

Cover and back illustration by Nik Payne.

Some names have been changed to protect the privacy of the individual.

Published by BookLocker.com, Inc., St. Petersburg, Florida.

Printed on acid-free paper.

BookLocker.com, Inc.
2018

First Edition

Praise for "All About Ilyas"

"All About Ilyas" is the fascinating and touching story of a distrusting young child who had the good fortune to be raised by loving foster parents. Having lived a traumatic childhood, Ilyas could be a bright and loving child one minute and an out of control, self-destructive one the next, set off by the slightest thing. Written from the journals his foster mother kept with excerpts from Ilyas' writing and art, adds dimension, humor and sadness to the story. It is written from her soul and the reader experiences her frustration, and near-hopelessness as well as humor and success on Ilyas' journey. Every parent, psychologist and teacher should read this book to get insight into child behavior and methods for handling a difficult child.

Linda Payne Smith
Creative Writing Instructor
Educator for 48 years

I could not stop reading this book and just finished. I am full of so many emotions right now, but the most powerful one is love. It was amazing from start to finish and left me wanting more.

Christy Foster – Teacher

I was so moved by your very special documentary of Ilyas. I began reading and never stopped until I finished. I think it would be a wonderful and educational book for anyone thinking of becoming a foster parent.

Mendy Wynn – Social Worker

I have read this book three times and I cried every time. This is a powerful and important story.

Christine Rosa – Educator

My experience has been that parents don't want to tell the difficult side of foster care because we don't like hearing "You brought this on yourself."
There are not enough people who understand that we can love doing foster care and hate it at the same time. Not want to do it anymore but do it anyway. There are not enough people who are willing to be uncomfortable for the sake of a child to have stability.

Lindsey Danielle – Foster Parent

This is a wonderful book. I could not stop once I started and read it right through. I am touched, impressed and more than a little emotional.

James Patton - Attorney

This book is dedicated to Ilyas;
The bravest person I know

Table of Contents

INTRODUCTION 1
MEETING ILYAS 3
JOURNAL ENTRY #1 (MONTH ONE) "I AM THE ADULT, YOU ARE THE CHILD" 6
JOURNAL ENTRY #2 (OCTOBER) BOUNDARIES 10
JOURNAL ENTRY #3 (NOVEMBER) THANKSGIVING 16
JOURNAL ENTRY #4 (DECEMBER) BIRTHDAY HEARTBREAK 21
JOURNAL ENTRY #5 (JANUARY- MONTH 5) CONSEQUENCES 25
JOURNAL ENTRY #6 (MONTH 6) BEGINNING OF THE END 30
JOURNAL ENTRY #7 (MARCH) THE GOLDEN RULE 37
JOURNAL ENTRY # 8 (APRIL, MONTH 8) WALKING ON LEGOS 42
JOURNAL ENTRY #9 (MONTH 9) THESE THINGS I BELIEVE 48
JOURNAL ENTRY # 10 (JUNE, MONTH 10) FUMING AND FURIOUS 55
JOURNAL ENTRY #11 (JULY) MY PERSONAL STRUGGLE 59
JOURNAL ENTRY # 12 (1 YEAR IN OUR HOME) THE DECISION 63
JOURNAL ENTRY #13 (SEPTEMBER) ONE STEP FORWARD 67
JOURNAL ENTRY #14 THE QUESADILLA DIET 70
JOURNAL ENTRY #15 (NOVEMBER) THEFT 74
JOURNAL ENTRY #16 (DECEMBER) BEING NINE 81
JOURNAL ENTRY # 17 (JANUARY, 17 MONTHS) "NO FUTURE FOR YOU" 85
JOURNAL ENTRY #18 (FEBRUARY) "YOU ARE MY STRONG MAN" 88
JOURNAL ENTRY #19 (18 MONTHS AT OUR HOME) A NORMAL KID 91
JOURNAL ENTRY #20 DAZED AND CONFUSED 95
JOURNAL ENTRY #21 A CAPACITY FOR EMOTION 98
JOURNAL ENTRY #22 (SUMMER) REGRETS 103
JOURNAL ENTRY #23 (FALL, 2 YEARS) PUPPY LOVE 106

JOURNAL ENTRY #24 (LATE FALL) ANTICIPATION	111
JOURNAL ENTRY #25 (WINTER) FAMILY TIME	115
JOURNAL ENTRY #26 (SPRING, 2 ½ YEARS) RECESS	118
JOURNAL ENTRY #27 (LATE SPRING) ANOTHER BIG CHANGE	120
JOURNAL ENTRY #28 (FALL/ WINTER, YEAR 3) FIFTH GRADE	125
JOURNAL ENTRY #29 (EARLY SPRING-11 YEARS OLD) TRAUMA AND TRUST	130
JOURNAL ENTRY #30 (LATE SPRING) SPORTS	135
JOURNAL ENTRY #31 (SUMMER) AGREEMENT BETWEEN MOTHER AND SON	139
JOURNAL ENTRY #32 FALL - 6TH GRADE PICK YOUR BATTLES	142
JOURNAL ENTRY # 33 WINTER - 6TH GRADE A VICTIM	148
JOURNAL ENTRY #33 SPRING - 6TH GRADE LOVE AND LEADERSHIP	152
JOURNAL ENTRY #35 (LATE SPRING -6TH GRADE) LOSS	157
JOURNAL ENTRY # 35 (SUMMER) WHAT DO WE DO NOW?	163
JOURNAL ENTRY #37 (AUGUST - FIVE YEARS WITH ILYAS) THE ANNOUNCEMENT	165
JOURNAL ENTRY #38 (3 YEARS LATER) AND, ADOPTION	167
EPILOGUE	175
ACKNOWLEDGEMENTS	177

Introduction

It was a beautiful day in September when we met Ilyas, our seven-year-old foster son for the first time. This story is about becoming foster parents, raising a foster child, and working within the foster system. The system is broken. The children are broken. And raising a broken child in a broken system can feel futile.

Foster care is defined in the Code of Federal Regulations as the "24-hour substitute care for children outside their home." It was put into place primarily to protect children from abuse and neglect and place them in safe care until they could return to their original guardians. The children who are assigned and filtered into the system are there for a reason and those reasons stem rarely, if ever, from a positive situation.

Our foster son was no exception. He came to us scared, untrusting, angry, and emotionally fragile. He had been abandoned, beaten, abused and molested. He had been in and out of the system for most of his short seven years.

We had no idea then of the change that would come into our lives. Ilyas' story is not the only narrative about the foster system, but his tale is singular and special within the lives of our family and is very personal for me. The journey of both his achievements and failures within his attempt to find his place in this world can serve as an example of how truly successful foster care can be for the people who choose to take it on. I hope my words lead to optimism and hope for any foster parent who find themselves in a similar situation as us and need an extra nudge of positivity to get through another day.

Foster parenting is not an easy task. Taking care of a troubled child can be exhausting and heartbreaking, giving way to frustration and desperation at the thought of things never changing or improving. What I hope to express though, is that becoming a foster parent may be the most rewarding journey a person can ever take. It can lead to a happiness experienced only by someone who has been through the darkness and stepped into the light.

We lived in a small town nestled in a valley in the mountains, just beyond the reach of the enormity of the Pacific Ocean. Our four children were born and raised here, and we had lived in our home for over thirty years. My husband, Biff, was a fire captain in a large city an hour away.

Children had always been a constant fixture in my life. I owned and operated a preschool. I taught parenting classes and coached middle and high school sports. My schooling and experience is in early childhood education.

At our home we had a large lawn, perfect for playing soccer and volleyball. We also had a big playground structure with a giant sandbox for digging and building. We were a very social family. We loved to host get-togethers, and our place was always full of love and laughter. We had opened our house to many kids over the years; there was always someone knocking on the door.

Throughout our time with Ilyas, I kept a journal. A space to vent my worries and frustrations. I wanted to keep close track of what was working and what wasn't working in the day-to-day interactions Ilyas had with our family and the community around him. Within this journal, I found the passion to provide a better life for the child in my care.

This book is written both from my actual journal entries and then in reflection of events after several years have passed. While this is a mother's perspective, it is also written and contemplated on by my experience and the many hours spent teaching, coaching and parenting.

Meeting Ilyas

Ilyas was first introduced to us in September and his presence brought an immediate whirlwind of new and unforeseen emotions for us as a family. We hadn't known quite what to expect. Biff and I had been licensed for about a month when we received the initial call from our FFA (Foster Family Agency) about a child in a neighboring county whom they had been unable to place. Our social worker told us this call was pretty much a last-ditch effort to find a family for a difficult boy who was otherwise going to be sent to a group home for more specialized care. They were pretty vague about any specifics regarding his case, and I only really remember being told this child was on several medications and was "cute." Our social worker did make us aware that the boy we were about to encounter could be a potentially difficult case but gave no reasons as to why. The information that foster parents receive never goes beyond the basics of the child's situation.

Regardless of the hazy details, Biff and I were curious about Ilyas. We were aware that protocol required us to meet and observe the child before making any long-term decisions. We agreed to meet with Ilyas if only to figure out whether he would be compatible with our family. We scheduled a meeting at his great-grandparent's house, about 45 minutes away.

Before meeting Ilyas, the idea of being a foster parent was only that - an idea. As it turns out, in my memory of meeting Ilyas, I realize that it characterizes one of the first moments where we felt the gravity of what we were planning to take on and what our decision would entail. There was very little tangibility to the idea of taking in a child, no matter how prepared we felt about the process. Regardless of any introductory training and paperwork Biff and I had gone through to get ready, being actively introduced to a boy we could potentially take under our wing was an entirely new experience.

On the scheduled date of the meeting, we drove separately, with Biff arriving first. The story begins with what he remembers, starting with his first sight of Ilyas as he pulled into the driveway.

He initially sighted Ilyas standing in the second story window frame, with his nose pressed to the glass, searching the landscape below him. Biff could practically feel the aura of longing and excitement from this child as he stood sentry at the window. His patient, watchful pose gave Biff the feeling that this boy must have been waiting for some time, but as soon as his car came to a stop, Ilyas was gone from the frame in an instant, only to come flying out the front door seconds later, arms stretched wide in ecstatic celebration.

"Dad! Dad! You've finally come!"

I distinctly remember Biff telling me about that moment, the surprise and sudden deluge of responsibility of having a child run at him with such hope and happiness, as well as the shock that came from a complete stranger calling him Dad.

All previous conceptions of what this meeting would entail were tossed out the window in those first seconds and Biff felt himself inundated with a new sense of responsibility not apparent moments before. It was in those first few minutes that he realized what becoming a foster parent was really going to involve. We were truly applying to be parents again. No matter how temporary the stay or how many children could come to us, we would be responsible for the care of a child in so many more ways than just physical. We also had a psychological and emotional duty to their well-being.

When I showed up at the house a short time later, I found Ilyas curled up with Biff on the couch. This picturesque scene was definitely not something I expected, and it caught me off guard. I could feel my emotions toward the situation becoming immediately amplified at the sight of the affectionate little boy before me and I knew that I was already being transformed. One of the main questions running through my head when I first saw Biff with Ilyas was, how does one respond to this? How can anyone do anything except take him in?

I often felt myself come back to this thought through my first year with Ilyas and remembering makes it easy to see what a pivotal moment that first meeting was for both Biff and me. It's one thing to go through the steps of becoming licensed as foster parents, but it is something entirely different when there is a living, breathing child in front of you and the hope and happiness sweeping its way through him becomes a palpable sensation.

For me, it erased any hesitation or uncertainty I might have carried when I walked into the room and he called me 'Mom'. I was charmed and taken in by his affection and enthusiasm, yet at the same time I knew that this was not totally normal behavior. I guess there was no meeting, no observation time or sleeping on it. We knew we were going to take that kid home with us.

At that time, the foster agency had not told Biff or me much regarding Ilyas' past, nor which particular issues could potentially arise in the event he came to live with us. The only facts made clear to us were that Ilyas was placed high up on the list of kids needing the most state care and that he was slated to be moved into a group home unless we agreed to take him.

We found ourselves in a binding position emotionally from the beginning. We felt an instant connection from our introduction with Ilyas and we were rather blindsided by the seemingly happy seven-year-old who wanted so very much to believe that Biff and I were his new parents coming to take him home at last.

Obviously, we knew that we might have our work cut out for us, but his quick attachment to us was exhilarating and exciting and it brought with it a hope that if he came to live with our family it would be, for him, a welcome transition into a fresh, new life. In more ways than one, I felt like it was no longer a matter of choice once we laid our eyes on Ilyas. The attachment was fast and solid, and left our family with no question. We quickly and confidently welcomed our new foster child with open arms.

Journal Entry #1 (Month One)
"I Am The Adult, You are The Child"

Ilyas came to live with us this month. He was very excited! He has a ton of energy and a super engaging smile. He loves his bunk beds and likes to think he has four beds - he can sleep on either bed at either end. He likes all the toys in his room but cannot play by himself. Actually, I think he loves the concept of all the toys and playthings. He wants someone to play everything with him. Ilyas loves the big yard, or the idea of the big yard. I have to prompt him to play by telling him to make something in the sandbox for five minutes or swing for six minutes. Then he can begin the activity and often sticks with it longer.

Ilyas touches everything but cannot stay with any activity for very long. He loves video games and will play those alone, although reluctantly. He eats everything we make and doesn't seem to be a picky eater! He sleeps well and cooperates at bedtime. Almost too compliant. I am used to meals and bedtimes being areas of contention with most kids and he is overly agreeable, which is concerning.

This first month we are working on BOUNDARIES. He has none. No physical, verbal or emotional boundaries. He has no sense of authority or who is in charge. He feels he is on the same level as the adults and has the same power as adults. I know this is a survival skill but doesn't work within our family dynamics.

Here at our house, Ilyas is the youngest of our brood. Their ages range from 16-28 with only Zak (age 16) living at home. He thinks he is on the same level as I am. I remind him constantly that he is the child, I am the adult. He feels he can tell me what to do, and I will obey him. Tough love time has just kicked in!

His mantra to learn is "I am the child, you are the adult." He doesn't say it willingly, but my hope is, it will sink in. I want to relieve him of the pressure of thinking he is the adult. Just be a kid. I want him to play, be silly, and act like a seven-year-old. I'll be the adult.

What I realized by the end of the first month was that every hour of every day was "All About Ilyas."

> I felt amamzed when I came to my house.
> I was wondering who is Zak?
> I was so amalazed that they had almost all the videgames.
> I was so amazed at my area
> It was so cool I thouht
>
> Plus a bunk bed and almost all the movies you cdid posabley want.

Ilyas 7 years old

Just as I am keeping a journal, I wanted Ilyas to have a chance to write down his own thoughts. I wanted him to be able to look back and see his time with our family through his own words. His thoughts, though rather simplistic, expressed excitement in a way any young boy would be excited; it focused only on the new objects at his disposal, and I found myself cheered by the fact he was expressing happiness in any form for his new placement. The process of becoming a foster parent is as rigorous as most people suspect. There are piles of paperwork, home visits, reference checks, security clearances and checklists. To receive a certificate of approval, we had to complete thirty hours of training that covered everything from foster children's rights to biological family rights. They try to cover every behavioral issue that may pop up. I enrolled in the classes twice.

We started the process with the county where we lived, but it was obvious they were overworked and understaffed. It was discouraging, and we didn't finish the paperwork, though we finished the classes, did the background check and got fingerprinted. We intended to pursue it again, when several months later, we were contacted by a Foster Family Agency (FFA). These are private agencies. They actively sought us out and made the process a bit easier. The social workers there have fewer caseloads, and in general more time to visit, and help with meetings and paperwork. The downside is they get the children the counties can't place for one reason or another. Often these are kids with behavior problems, multiple failed placements or special needs. That is how we got Ilyas from a different county than the one we lived in.

We were, for the most part, unaware of much of Ilyas' past. Most of what we were to learn came from him, and bits and pieces from the social workers. Ilyas was considered an Intensive Treatment Foster Child (ITFC) and was deemed non-placeable because of behavior issues, failed placements and medications he was on. We were not told exactly what these behavior issues were, why he failed placements or why he was on the meds.

At the time we met Ilyas, he was living at his great-grandparents' house. He called them Tikun and Tipau. He had been moved across the state, so he could be closer to the only biological family he had. His Tikun and Tipau were in their eighties and couldn't care for him full time so they put him back into foster care. Every time he failed another placement (and there were several), the county would place him back with them until they could find a new home. His great-grandparents were caring and loving but couldn't keep up with the demands and issues of a child that was so damaged by his past.

When he arrived at our home he was just over four feet tall and weighed only fifty pounds, well below average for a seven-year-old. We were told his last placement had been a failed fost-adopt home. His fost-adopt parents had called him in on a mental health hold (5150) and he was sent to the children's ward in a psychiatric hospital.

After we agreed to the placement and took him home, they gave us more specifics on his hospitalization. He was diagnosed with Reactive Attachment Disorder or RAD, attention deficit hyperactivity disorder (ADHD) and depression. He was given two psychotropic drugs - one for depression (100mg of Seroquel daily and another 100 mg at night) and one for manic/schizophrenic behaviors (10 mg of Lexapro daily). He also took 28 mg of Strattera for ADHD. These are all adult doses and he weighed only 50 pounds!

This was my first inkling into the system and how it treated foster children with behavior problems. It seemed inconceivable that any child so young could warrant such large doses of medication. I was at the same time worried that he was a danger to himself and others, and worried that we had taken on a child with such extreme mental health issues, that I dare not miss a dose!

I did know this: no child with an intact family or parental guidance would ever allow such medications to be given to their own child. One item Biff and I brought to the table early on with regards to being foster parents, was that we were going to raise our foster children with the same opportunities and principles with which we raised our biological children. I honestly think that I quickly formed an even deeper attachment to this boy because no-one seemed to care enough about him to stop his downward spiral. He needed love and stability to pull him back up and put his feet firmly on the ground.

We quickly learned Ilyas had an exceptional mind and was a master at manipulation. He read voraciously and could lose himself in a book instantly. He had already read the Harry Potter book series and had a fascination with ancient mythology.

From the onset, Ilyas felt a connection to Biff, and for the most part was better behaved around him. It could have been due to the fact that Biff was six feet five inches tall with an intimidating build, but it seemed Ilyas knew him for what he was. A burly giant with a tender heart. Ilyas fell in love quickly with our 16-year-old son, Zak. He idolized him and followed him everywhere! Our daughter Zoe, attended college out of town, and siblings Billy and Bekah were finished with college and living in San Diego. Ilyas was able to see them often and quickly memorized their phone numbers so he could call them whenever he wanted. Which he often did. Mostly, when he was angry or distraught. Usually with me.

Journal Entry #2 (October)
Boundaries

Two months with Ilyas in our home and he is settling in and feeling more comfortable. He doesn't like his name or explaining how to pronounce it. We nicknamed him "S". He loves it and asks everyone to call him S.

We are working on boundaries. All boundaries! Physical, verbal and emotional. Physical boundaries are tangible, like a fence or border. He is often found in inappropriate places, such as behind the checkout counter, on top of shelves, or under store racks. Imagining invisible walls is something Ilyas either doesn't understand or chooses not to understand.

Another boundary we continually work on is staying out of people's personal space. I'll tell him, "This is my box, my personal space, and I don't always want you in it!" I have given him another nickname - "Underfoot."

Ilyas inserts himself into every interaction, every conversation. He butts in whether it involves him or not. He then turns the subject to be about him. He is learning boundaries, albeit reluctantly.

INSIDE EMOTIONS! Keep some thoughts inside your head. "There is no need to verbalize everything you think or feel." He has a constant dialogue of "I'm cold, I'm hot, I'm tired, I'm hungry, I'm bored, I'm starving." It is basic complaining 101 and the constant grumbles are exhausting. We are also working on adding filters. He tends to blurt out things like "He is fat" or "That lady has a big nose." There's nothing like a kid that finds himself in the wrong place at the wrong time and then tops it off by spouting something rude or offensive.

Ilyas likes his new school. He is in second grade and rides the bus. He didn't go to preschool or kindergarten and didn't even attend first grade for the whole year. He plays with our neighbor who is also in second grade and it is great to have a friend live nearby.

He is beginning to get better about playing by himself, but still wants A LOT OF ATTENTION! At all times in all venues...it's "All About Ilyas."

Attention is what Ilyas wants more than anything. It is tiring and exhausting for me. Yesterday was a fairly typical day in my life with Ilyas.

The afternoon begins with me picking him up after school. I let him play for an hour at the after-school YMCA so I expected a happy boy. On the way to the car he begins complaining about his day. The kids, his teacher, the yard duty were all mean to him. I acknowledge I hear him, but don't start a conversation.

"Hmm," is all I say.

Then he rants on about the weather, the curve in the road, the leaves on the ground. I turn up the radio to try to drown him out. He keeps on. There is no point in engaging with him. It is an argument I can't win...because there is no real argument. If I ask him to stop complaining, he'll ramp up, not down.

We stop at the grocery store. Maybe this will distract him. Nope! He rams the cart into shelves and knocks over some canned goods. He barely misses clipping someone elderly. He drops fruit on the ground.

"Oops!" he says.

"Ilyas, stop! Seriously!" I am getting frustrated.

Then he begins to whine because I wouldn't buy him a jump rope. We get home. I ask him to help carry in the bags. He whines, fusses and then drops a bag in the driveway. He falls down, cries and tells me he's hurt. I ask him to hang up his backpack.

"No!" It ends up on the floor.

"Okay, how about moving it to your room?"

"No!"

"Please, Ilyas!"

"No. I don't want to."

I let it go. I need to pick my battles and the afternoon was already shaping up to be a doozy. I head outside to water and feed the animals. He follows me, complaining the entire time.

"Please, Ilyas. I need a minute. Go play"
"No. I don't want to."
"What do you want?" No reply.

I start dinner. My shadow is right there. He kicks over the cat food, pees on the toilet seat, pulls down the papers on the desk. I ignore him. He gets louder, spins around, dancing, jumping on and off the couch.

"Are you hungry?" No reply.

"Are you trying to make me mad at you?" I ask. No reply.

Finally, I give up. I sit down, hold him and we tell stories. Dinner is late, the house is cold, but he is content. For now.

Ilyas – 7 years old

It was tempting to sweep Ilyas' inability to be by himself under the rug. Maybe he was simply being subjected to too many new things at once, thus becoming over stimulated as any child might. I knew from being a parent and teacher that this craving for attention is quite natural in any young child. However, I found myself beginning to consider why Ilyas had this excessive need for constant attention. Although he had only been with us a couple of months, I could clearly see that he did not like to be left alone. He needed someone to play with him and watch over him at all times. The way he kept his eyes glued to us, even while he played, made me think he seemed afraid he would be forgotten if he were left on his own for any period of time.

The need for attention manifests itself even more so with foster children. Most foster children have experienced a form of abuse or neglect at the hands of their parents or previous guardians. Many of these kids experience difficulties with boundaries or lack thereof because they did not grow up in a home where rules of behavior were established. Fending for themselves, these kids didn't learn appropriate social cues, because their parents were abusive, absent or both. This lack of knowledge puts neglected children at a higher risk of growing up with an array of issues stemming from insecurities, and uncertainty that they feel both within themselves and with the world around them. As I watched Ilyas maneuver the household during these first months in our lives, I soon found he was no exception to this problem.

I found myself using the phrase "All About Ilyas" throughout my journal because it seemed appropriate in so many ways. From the moment he arrived, he needed every eye in the house focused on him. In fact, the idea of the world revolving around Ilyas became a running slogan within the family. I latched onto this phrase because I believed that Ilyas' issues with neediness and attention were the main reasons for many of the problems he experienced with us and probably past placements. Once I began to understand the world through his eyes, I could then help shape his behaviors in a more appropriate way.

Regardless of these early problems or annoyances, most of my initial feelings on the move-in were still overwhelmingly positive. We met Ilyas' arrival with plentiful optimism because we were confident he would reach a comfortable stride once he got used to his new routine. He could be extremely moody, hyper, and inappropriate at times, but he was also cheerful and seemingly happy. The animated, upbeat

Ilyas was like any other child at that young age. That gave us hope that he would outgrow his negative behaviors with guidance and time. After all, Biff and I shared more than enough experience between us with raising our own children and teaching and coaching others. We honestly believed we would see a turnaround that was, if not quick, at least not unnecessarily long and complicated.

While I knew the initial excitement couldn't last, I didn't want to begin to doubt that we'd made the right decision. At the beginning, every time Ilyas looked at me and grinned, it validated our commitment. He had an amazing smile that could light up a room and the affection he poured into our family was gratifying and infectious.

However, uncertainty began to grow in me after the first couple of months. Pretty soon I noticed he was regressing further into more demanding behavior. The honeymoon period was over. He quickly went to his dark moods that drained me of all joy and happiness. How could such a little guy be so capable of creating and changing the tone so completely? As I noticed early on, he was a master of manipulation and if he didn't like what was happening, everyone around him knew it. He complained nonstop, about e-v-e-r-y-thing! Keep it to yourself. Inside emotions.

At first, I wasn't exactly sure how to address his constant demand of attention. I did love the fact he was comfortable enough to express himself. I didn't want to take that away from him, but I wanted him to learn more positive and considerate forms of communication. Whenever he interrupted someone or steered the conversation toward himself, I pointed out that all people were special, had their own talents and gifts and deserved to have their voices heard. The main problem was that Ilyas always had to be THE BEST at everything, the cutest, the fastest, the smartest. He had an extremely hard time thinking about how others felt or why their emotions were important. He did not have the ability to sit and listen while someone else shared their thoughts. I became concerned about his inability to recognize and feel empathy. His all-consuming need for attention left no room for considering other people's thoughts, feelings, or emotions.

I thought maybe if he felt he was the best at everything, and the greatest kid ever, then maybe there would be no cause for him to feel unwanted. The worth he felt for himself was clearly interconnected with how he saw others perceiving him. He needed the family to pay attention to him and that made him feel important and wanted. If he wasn't getting enough attention, then he may be lost forever.

Part of the reason Ilyas so obsessively craved attention was because he felt both terrified and sure it would eventually go away. He felt skeptical that the care our family showed him would continue as we got used to him. Maybe our feelings for him would fade if he was quiet or compliant.

To Ilyas, attention from us meant we cared.

If our attention toward him diminished, he would be left alone again in a society which had continuously seemed to abandon him. In his brief experience of life, everyone had abandoned him or given up on him. His fear of abandonment may also account for his inappropriate comments and actions and the frequency with which he chose to misbehave, even when corrected. He could easily see the rise it would get out of me when he behaved negatively, and my reactions encouraged him because, even though I was angry, he could be absolutely sure I was listening to him! At that time, he didn't seem to care about differentiating between positive and negative attention. Instead he just lumped it all together, satisfied to receive unbroken focus in any form.

Journal Entry #3 (November)
Thanksgiving

Three months in. Ilyas is eating and sleeping well. He really is getting better at remembering physical boundaries. I just have to say "boundaries" and he immediately complies. He is less of a shadow, still always tagging along, but not so much in our space.

I wondered about all the meds he is taking. One morning after forgetting to give him his doses, I drove to his school to give him his meds. I was nervous about how he might act without them. If he is this disruptive and moody on them, what if he missed a dose? I was afraid to find out. What exactly do these meds do? I need to ask his psychiatrist this question.

We went shopping for a birthday present for ten-year-old cousin Joey. Ilyas seemed excited to pick the gift out. After helping choose a gift, he threw a fit in the store because HE didn't get anything. He yelled, screamed and started grabbing things off the shelves. I literally had to drag him out to the car. Turned out he didn't want Joey to get a present if he couldn't get one too.

We talked a lot about the feeling of giving and how wonderful that feels. I started using that dialogue whenever he did his chores or did a favor for someone. I would tell him that helping is a form of giving and it feels great. Right? He fights the feeling...but I can see him beginning to at least think about it.

He is starting to have a hard time with his peers at school. While giving is difficult for him, taking is easy! He has started taking things he wants and even things he doesn't want. Almost daily I'm getting notes or calls from the school or his after school YMCA about him taking pencils, markers, books and playground balls.

Thanksgiving was a nightmare! Our large extended family was there and Ilyas could not handle it. He wasn't the center of attention and tried and tried to get attention any way he could. He finally flipped out big time...kicked, yelled, punched and tore apart the room he was sent to.

All this over not getting something he wanted; a turn at a video game. Having the whole family there seemed to only make for a bigger audience. I understand the holidays can be tough, but AGAIN his behavior came down to wanting all the attention. In the middle of all his anger, he flipped right back to this happy kid once the family decided to go to a movie. He was considerate and affectionate. The family though, was still reeling from his behavior. I was still upset, embarrassed, exhausted and would have gladly gone without him, but his champion, and patient oldest brother Billy, took over and sat by him and (whew!) all ended well.

It was time to impose consequences for actions. We started to take away privileges such as TV and video games and started restricting his playtime with friends. But first he needed to write an apology letter to the family.

I think it is important to recognize since this was Ilyas' first holiday with the extended family, it would be natural he would have some difficulty fitting in. Especially with a large influx of people who were strangers to him and yet so familiar to one another. He may have felt ignored by the family interacting with other loved ones they had not seen in a while. It is obvious that he felt a heavy sense of injustice at not receiving all of the family's attention and chose to act out in any way he could in order to gain back the focus he had momentarily lost. He resorted to loud temper outbursts to make everyone else aware of him, oblivious to the kind of attention he received.

The fact that the afternoon ended with the family going to a movie served to prove to him he was still gaining rewards even when acting out negatively. When I sent him to a separate room after his melt down, it did little good, and the only thing that finally seemed to placate him was the promise of a movie. However, although Ilyas may have felt this day was a win for him, I didn't let this behavior get past me, and began to focus on the importance for implementing real consequences. I was also aware that it would mean looking at the root or cause of Ilyas' behavioral issues first.

My journal entry about the shopping trip clearly demonstrates Ilyas' quick escalation as soon as something didn't go the way he wanted. His behavior began to intensify and grow increasingly dark every time he didn't get his way. It could be over what he wanted to eat, a show he wanted to watch or a place he wanted to go. If he was told no, he flew into an uncontrollable tantrum instead of being able to process the rejection in a more appropriate form.

Note to self: REJECTION = Trigger #1

Ilyas expects to have the power of an adult. The obvious problem with this is that it undermines my authority if he believes I have no right to tell him what or what not to do. At one point he even said outright that I had no right to boss him around because I was "just a woman."

This aversion to, and challenging of authority, is not uncommon with foster children. These kids often experience trouble taking orders from people they consider strangers or temporary figures in their life. Refuting authority is a tactic many children use because it makes them feel more powerful and in control of a situation. Control combats against the insecurities and powerlessness they often feel about their general circumstances in society.

In the hopes of warding off any misconceptions about who was in charge of whom, I repeatedly asked him to verbalize the mantra he learned a couple of months ago; " I am the child— YOU are the adult." I hoped that, by making this concept crystal clear, I could curb his inappropriate outbursts before they began. I was aware, however, that this was only a minor step and that changing Ilyas' behavior was something which would not happen overnight, and maybe not as quickly as I originally hoped. There was a long road ahead for us and I was just beginning to see the first signs on the pathway.

Ilyas began to talk about his past. He told us that he remembered being left in his crib for hours and no one came to get him or feed him. He recalled climbing out of his crib to find food and the only food he could reach was Nesquik chocolate milk powder. In his mind there were memories of a man repeatedly beating his parent and also beating him. He remembered when and where he was hit with a stick, a belt and a hanger and he has the scars to prove it. He told us that this man was taken away in a police car because of drugs and stolen money. He witnessed all this, usually hiding behind the couch.

Ilyas didn't go to preschool or play outside. His mom had a drug problem and the apartment they lived in was shared by strangers and other drug users. His mom was gone or passed out much of the time. He told us he was hit often. Yet, when he could, he took care of her. He said he was scared all the time.

He only shared bits and pieces at a time, but it was clear he had begun to trust us more. He was opening up his heart, which in turn made him feel vulnerable. He wanted to be tough all the time and it was refreshing to see a softer, tender side to him.

He had also asked us to please adopt him. <u>Adopt</u> him!? We signed up to be foster parents only and it broke a little of me when I had to tell him we couldn't adopt him. We had no plans to adopt anyone.

The biggest single influence in Ilyas' life at that time was Zak. Zak at sixteen, and a junior in high school, was the only one still living at home. Ilyas adored him, idolized him and listened to him. If Zak was disappointed or frustrated with him, it carried much more weight than it did for us, the parents. Ilyas followed Zak everywhere.

They often went on hikes and adventures. We lived in a rural community with several state parks close by. Ilyas didn't have any experience with being outside in nature and often complained. But Zak just kept on walking and talking and soon he began to look forward to these excursions. While Zak was patient and understanding, he also called Ilyas out on everything. If they were playing video games and he started to whine or cheat, Zak would just get up, turn off the TV and walk away.

I didn't have that luxury as a parent.

I couldn't just turn the problem off and walk away. For the most part I felt like I always had to deal with the issue at hand and every issue was a life lesson to be learned.

His first report card and parent teacher conference happened this month. The results were a little discouraging. He received a passing grade in homework, but all the rest were unsatisfactory or inconsistent. At our conference, I got the feeling his teacher was trying hard to find the positives wherever she could. She was a great teacher and he was already wearing her out!

Journal Entry #4 (December)
Birthday Heartbreak

Ilyas turned eight this month! We had a birthday party for him at Chuck E. Cheese. We waited and waited but no kids from school showed up. He was so sad and looked so dejected. He asked several times when his friends would arrive, and finally went off and sat in a corner. Then suddenly, he jumped up and ran around the place like he was on fire! He laughed loudly, touched everything and wouldn't listen to anyone. He wouldn't even settle down to play a game. He was trying so hard to be cheerful, yet I knew his little heart was breaking. We ended up leaving and he was quiet the whole way home. He told me that was his first birthday party he ever had and thanked us.

Today he was sent home from school and suspended for three days. He was aggressive toward some kids and called another child a mother f#@*x. He has started to lose recess time at school and sits in the office most days. He is becoming verbally aggressive, disrespectful and he is telling stories that aren't true. Right now, he is not very likeable, and he seems dark and angry. We are being super firm at home. We insist he take responsibility for EVERY action and he doesn't like it.

After the incident at Thanksgiving, we needed to make arrangements for him to stay over Christmas break at his great grandparents' house. We had planned a trip to Mexico and we couldn't take the chance of having him wreck another family holiday. It was stressful even thinking about taking him. We went to Mexico with our other four children. It was a great break...the kids are wondering if fostering this guy is working.

We celebrated Christmas with Ilyas before we left for Mexico, but his heart wasn't in it. He knew we were going without him, and he knew why. I felt bad for his elderly great grandparents, but it was a necessary lesson for Ilyas and a break for us. He put up a good front when we picked him up, but I knew he was hurt because we left him behind.

Trigger #2 = Abandonment

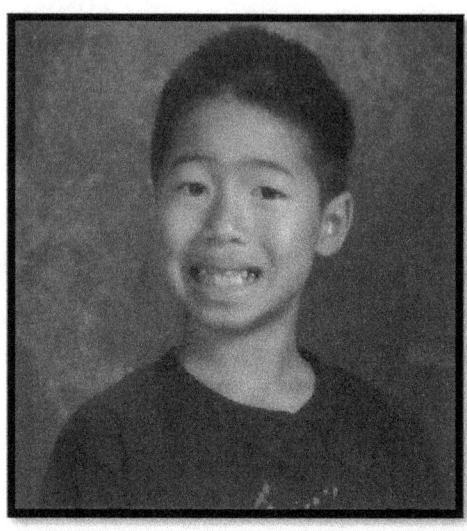

Ilyas had been diagnosed with Reactive Attachment Disorder (RAD), which meant that he didn't have a chance to attach to a loving and committed adult during his first eighteen months of life. It is through attachment with a loving and protective caregiver that a young child learns to love and trust others, to become aware of others' feelings and needs, to regulate emotions, and to develop healthy relationships and a positive self-image. The absence of emotional warmth during the first few years of life can negatively affect a child's entire future.

The parent is really an extension of what the baby needs to create a sense of self. Parents or caregivers bring food, warmth, movement and laughter to a child. In a healthy bond between mother and child there are thousands of emotionally rich moments that feed the sensory aspects of an infant's brain. They promote reciprocal moments of touch, smiles, eye contact, and facial expressions. Healthy attached infants have their needs met. When they cry they are comforted. When they are hungry they are fed, and when they smile they are rewarded with smiles and hugs.

When an infant's world is constantly lacking in these attachment experiences, their emerging sense of self is diminished, and they experience a pervasive sense of worthlessness. Rather than feel joy and excitement, the child feels despair and terror when their needs are not met. The world to them seems cold, unresponsive and unpredictable. They haven't been able to consistently bounce emotions off a caregiver. When they have needs, they often cry, and scream in rage, unable to understand what they need, and why no one is attending to them.

"Fredericks Experiment"

In the thirteenth century, the German king, Frederick II, conducted a diabolical experiment intended to discover what language children would naturally grow up to speak if never spoken to. He thought it would be German which would make his race the supreme race. King Frederick took babies from their mothers at birth and placed them in the care of nurses who were forbidden to speak in their presence. A second rule was also imposed. The nurses were not allowed to touch the infants. They were fed and diapered in silence with as little touch as possible. To his great dismay, Frederick's experiment was cut short, but not before something tragically significant regarding human nature was revealed. The babies grew up to speak no language at all because they died. They all died before the age of one. (Digma.com)

We now call this "failure to thrive." We know how important it is to have an attentive, consistent caregiver but what happens when the caregiver is inconsistent? The child can end up like Ilyas - poorly attached, with all the ramifications that brings. Discipline is experienced with rejection and contempt. They will always seek to control their environment since they cannot relax and expect the adult will naturally keep them safe and will meet their needs. This is a matter of survival!

"Attachment Disorder is defined as the condition in which individuals have difficulty forming lasting relationships. They often show nearly a complete lack of ability to be genuinely affectionate with others. They typically fail to develop a conscience and do not learn to trust."

(www.attachment.org/reactive attachment-disorder)

I recognized this lack of attachment in Ilyas. He was a textbook case and if left alone, he would probably grow up to have deep issues and problems. Trust, confidence and self-esteem would be beyond his grasp and he would push away those that got too close.

Many years ago, I worked with brain-injured children and the buzz word then was "patterning." We would take the children back to infancy and attempt to reprogram their brains by providing all the developmental steps they may have missed. We passively moved their limbs through physical developments like creeping, crawling, walking, running and jumping. We repeated these exercises over and over until the brain believed it had happened, and these kids could catch up on missed developmental milestones. Even though the method has been replaced and new research has changed the process, I thought a similar method could work with the lack of attachment for Ilyas.

I felt if I could replicate what he missed in infancy, that part of his brain development might reboot. I took him back to infancy. I sat and cradled him tight. I read to him, laughed when he made a joke and smiled when he smiled. I tousled his hair and played games with him. I attended to his needs quickly. When he was hungry, I fed him. When he was upset, I comforted him. I tried to show him I was deeply engaged in understanding him. Empathizing with his distress, I tried not to criticize and constantly evaluate him.

I wanted to show him the joy and safety that lies within being part of a good family. That is much easier said than done!

How do you try to engage in reciprocal enjoyment when you are met with a sullen, angry and dejected child? Here's how; I told him the truth. I told him what I was doing and why. I told him he missed out on a lot of important milestones growing up and we were going to recreate them. He and I together. I told him none of that was his fault, and I was sorry it happened to him. He cried. I cried. He showed vulnerability but deep down I knew he was terrified about what would happen when he left our house. He knew from experience, no placement lasted very long.

Journal Entry #5 (January- Month 5)
Consequences

Ilyas is taking swimming lessons. He can't swim a stroke, and we are a water loving family that surfs and swims. He is learning, although he sinks, so his swimming looks like a controlled drown. We got him a bike for Christmas. Excited to show off, he yelled, "Mom watch me!" Then he got on and rode wildly down the street and crashed into the neighbor's garage. Soooo..we worked on braking and control. I taught him how to skid and challenged him to make a longer and longer skid line. Within a week he mastered the brakes, learned to steer and could ride around the block.

We wanted to start January off on a clean slate. I make an effort to let the little things go and pick my battles. I try to disengage and not be continually on him about his behavior. At the same time, I am receiving repeated phone calls from the school and the after-school YMCA program about his behavior. He's either sullen and distant or angry and aggressive. It is exhausting and depressing to hear this from teachers and staff, and when he gets home, I see more of the same behaviors. Ilyas has started lying. He lies about everything, even things he doesn't need to lie about. "Zak was really mean to me and wouldn't play with me and grabbed and twisted my arm." Ilyas stated. He hadn't even seen Zak all day.

I had to think of a consequence that mattered. Sending him to his room didn't work. He either fell asleep or tore the room apart, and then there had to be a consequence for that! I really needed to have him make sense of what he was doing, why he did it, and learn how to curb the bad behavior before it escalated. Poorly attached children respond best to discipline that involve minimal choices and clear consequences. It seemed hard for him understand the connection between his actions or behavior and the consequences of that behavior.

I decided to have him write. Write about the things we talked about, about the lessons we were trying to teach him. Maybe writing it down would help it sink in. Choosing to write could earn him a day off restriction. I would take a page of his thoughts for a day of grounding. There has to be a light at the end of the tunnel for both of us! It was hard to be consistent, yet I knew in the end, consistency will serve him well. He hated being grounded so he began to write.

Writing became the perfect consequence. Sitting at his desk, armed with a dictionary, he had to define specific words, and use them in a sentence. He also had to write letters of apology - many letters! Turned out, he hated desk work. In order to find a good consequence, he had to hate it. His vocabulary was huge, because of his love of books, and he needed practice using these words and understanding them. I think I finally found the appropriate consequence for the action!

> January 08
> 2 definitions for RESPECT
> to turn to   high opinion
> or admiration of somebody
>
> 1/15/08 - after disrespecting mom and being destructive.
> 1 example of respecting your family
> respect people's proptey
>
> help your mom clean the yard
>
> 1 example of respecting your friends
> dont take your friends toys.
> dont take your friends tranformers.

The courts changed Ilyas' therapist to one closer to us. We were mandated to take him, and therapy would help if he were willing to be helped. He wasn't inclined to discuss any of his issues with any of them. With Ilyas being on the highest tier of care for foster kids, we were also given twenty hours a week for what were called "Support Counselors." These counselors can go into the classroom, or the after-school program and have a one-on-one with him. They are trainees, usually still in school for psychology majors or working on a thesis. The idea or concept seemed like a good one, but for us it backfired. Ilyas didn't want them there. In his mind they served as a daily reminder of the fact that he was a foster kid with problems. The counselors being at school embarrassed and humiliated him. It made him stand out as needy and special.

It didn't take long before he began to manipulate the support counselors to let him get out of class and play on the playground during school. If they stayed for the after-school program they let him win at games and played solely with him. He cooperated best with the male aids but could manipulate anyone. The counselors catered to him, feeling they were there to ward off any outbursts. While he didn't have as many altercations with his peers, he also didn't have as many interactions with them. He often had different workers, and none held firm to our wish that Ilyas must cooperate in the classroom, complete his work, and make friends.

Ilyas complained that we didn't love him, that we didn't want him, and that we were mean to him. He also talked about how he wasn't worth anything. He started to sabotage everything good that could happen and instead turn it into a negative, especially things that he had control over. He'd make plans to do something special, and then almost unconsciously decided he didn't deserve it.

He would get himself worked up and agitated as the event got closer. Then someone would end up hurt, something would get broken, or unkind words spoken so that I had to tell him he couldn't go. Which was a punishment for both of us!

Every day was a power struggle. He took toys from the YMCA. He was benched at recess all week for one thing or another, which didn't serve him well. He needed that activity and interaction with his peers. I got calls because he said the "F" word to kids. His teacher reported that he was being mean to his friends and saying really hurtful things.

The school asked to have a conference to see how to move forward with all of this. He did have an (Individualized Education Program) IEP, that had recently been replaced with a 504. A "504" is a plan developed to ensure that a child who has a disability identified under the law receives accommodations that will ensure their academic success. In his plan he was allowed to stand while working at his desk, have more freedom of movement and sit closer to the front. The principal and his teacher have been more than accommodating. His issues were really not learning related, but behavior problems.

Sorry, mom for saying I didn't like you. I won't do it again. I am sorry for what i did.

from, Ilyas

Journal Entry #6 (Month 6)
Beginning Of The End

<u>Early February</u>. Ilyas is lying, stealing and being disrespectful. We saw his psychiatrist and it helped to hear we are doing the right things. Sometimes it feels we are making no progress and putting out so much effort. Ilyas can wear you down. He is especially disrespectful toward women. Zak is also fed up with his behavior. Biff, who is a fireman and works overnights is gone a lot, but stills sees that Ilyas is affecting our lives negatively. We are a busy family and the constant stress of dealing with Ilyas is getting to us all. Again, if it is not "All about Ilyas" then he is mad.

We talk a lot about being optimistic. Ilyas is always looks for the negative in things. "Be careful what you wish for," I remind him constantly. He will complain that he'll never get new Legos, when what he really wants is to get new Legos. He will tell us that he will always be bad, when he is actually trying to be good. I ask him to voice what he really wants. Do you want a negative outcome, or do you want a positive outcome? Take a risk and hope! He needs to believe he can ask for something and won't be rejected. That is risky behavior on his part, because for him to verbalize a want or need makes him vulnerable and he sets himself up for rejection, which is his number one trigger.

On the positive side, his physical boundaries have all but been resolved and he can play inside or outside by himself. When he writes in his journal, I give him subjects that are not all about him and try to keep things on the positive side.

<u>The New Lesson</u> - Treat others the way you want to be treated. The golden rule. Not golden to Ilyas.

The stress of dealing with this little guy is starting to show. I have had to go on blood pressure medication. It would be easier not to deal with all his issues, but he is so worth the effort. HE is worth the effort but is IT worth the effort?

<u>Late February</u>. Is anything really helping?

Raising Ilyas is like dealing in opposites. Craving attention, his methods for getting it push you away. Ignoring him is often the best solution for all of us. To disengage from his constant arguments and complaints, works as a simmering down of what would become an escalated situation for him. Yet at the same time ignoring him is to not listen to him, to not engage with him which he so desperately needs.

As angry as he appears to be, it is good, that it seems to be all at the surface. He is getting over things quicker and not holding on to his anger. He has begun to show empathy toward others. Well at least he can tell someone else what they should feel or do. He has begun to recite our rules and philosophies to other kids in situations where there might be confrontation.

We honestly love this little boy! Working through all his problems will take time and patience.

That said, we have started the proceedings for him to leave our family. I think he needs a higher level of care and we are exhausted.

> 2- definitions for [DIS RESPECT]
> rude, impolite. lack of respect
> rudeness
>
> 1- example of [disrespecting] your family
> use impolite words with your mom.

Definition of disrespect

While I did initiate the process to have him moved, Ilyas knew nothing about it. I originally told the social workers we would commit for a year and that year is up in six months at the end of summer. I hope we can make it.

We attended to Ilyas' needs as best we could but the underlying issue with him (and most other foster kids) is trust. We trusted him, but I wondered if he would ever trust us? In his mind it was always just a matter of time before he would be removed from our home. That had been his experience so far.

Ilyas honestly loves where he is, and he loves us, and knows that leaving will hurt more the longer he is here. The worse he acts out, the quicker he gets moved. If he makes life too hard for us, he will be removed, and he will save himself from getting more attached to our family. He also knows the strain he is causing but can't seem to change the downward spiral.

If he could develop the trust that we care for him and will be there for him, he could hope for a different outcome. Building his trust means being consistent and reliable. Trust means you are meeting your child's' needs and also their desires.

He asks, "Will you please adopt me?"

I tell him again we can't. We aren't adopting anyone. We are just foster parents. But it breaks my heart. Again, rejection and abandonment are his main triggers and his request makes him vulnerable and my answer makes him angry. All my reassurances that we care for him fall on deaf ears, because to him, they are empty promises.

I am also beginning to see the effect of our community's attitude toward Ilyas, toward foster children. When broaching the topic of foster care, it is difficult to prevent certain images from popping up in people's minds. People conjure up exaggerated and dramatic ideas of the welfare system, based straight out of popular television crime shows.

Episodes are built on kids who run the streets, sell drugs, and are generally delinquent. Runaways and homeless kids are pushed into overworked systems with overworked foster parents and being spit out of them just as quickly. These children are generally seen as abused and forgotten, and in the back of society's mind is the nagging thought that they have little chance at a bright future or a warm home. It always struck me that the emotion hardly ever talked about and even more rarely felt, is hope.

I bring this up because I have encountered many people who feel negative toward foster children. It baffles and concerns me that these generalizations are so pervasive when they can be so harmful to the individuals they describe. The image of the irreparable troubled foster child is by no means a prerequisite of children within the system. I had many conversations with people that began with sympathy for Ilyas, but then they dismissed his aggressive acting out behavior as now unjustified. They think because, after all, he has a great place to live and a family to care for him, he should be thankful and appreciative.

Foster kids often appear as feeling entitled and unappreciative of new homes and environments. I understood that these kids didn't ask to be in the foster system. They didn't want to have to learn to love a new family or home. They wanted their own homes with their birth parents. These kids are in survival mode, and realistically know their lives are always in transition. Another home, different caregivers, another school, another neighborhood. They have to look out for themselves, and the walls they build around them are strong and not easily penetrated.

The poor attendance at Ilyas' birthday party made me sad and frustrated because at that point I wasn't entirely sure how to begin to turn the negativity around. I could tell that a real struggle was beginning to show, and it was one of the first times I saw how isolated Ilyas was from the community around him. His aggressive and unfavorable behavior toward people was turning him into a pariah. That in turn pushed him further within himself, rather than allowing him to branch out and interact in a healthy, positive way.

At this point, most of my attempts to correct and extinguish Ilyas' negative behavior have failed. Instead of becoming more comfortable and happy within his new environment, he was driving himself away and destroying any connections with those around him. Not only was this hindering my ability to teach him appropriate behavior, I also noticed this detachment made Ilyas feel more unwanted and uncomfortable, especially at school. He voiced these emotions when he came home and complained that so-and-so didn't like him. He could just feel it. Following his train of thought, I could see why he was having such a hard time. If the kids at school didn't want to be friends with him, why should he waste any effort attempting to be nice in return? A childish view, but he was a child. His behavior prevented him from forming friendships, both in and out of school, at home.

I began to notice that parents were reluctant or even refusing to let their children play with Ilyas because of the fear that his problems would rub off on their own children. As if he were a hardened delinquent rather than a little boy recently thrown into a new and foreign situation. Instead of showing understanding and sympathy toward Ilyas' past, I found that the people I interacted with shut down and rejected him outright merely because of his label as a "foster child."

Although this may sound like our personal situation, negative connotations such as these surround foster children and are not limited to us. The way these children are viewed has a greater permanent impact on them than people realize, and it begins earlier than many would care to admit. The negativity that surrounds labeling a foster child as troubled or unstable can follow them throughout their whole lives and shape how they view their own self-worth.

I think of "Anne of Green Gables," written over one hundred years ago. A little girl wants to befriend the newly adopted Anne, only to be admonished by her mother not to play with her, because she was an orphan.

"But she didn't ask to be an orphan," said the little girl.

"Of course not dear," replied her mother. "But she is."

which led to him being more depressed both in class and

It was easy to feel sad for this little guy when others teased him and bullied him, because when he came home I saw how vulnerable and fragile he really was. He put up a tough exterior, but that exterior was so thin. . . you could scrape it all away with a word or even a look. I could see how hard it was for him and how he didn't want other people to know how deeply it hurt him to be criticized and ostracized. Instead of talking to Biff and I about it, he withdrew to "That Place" inside himself where he could put up a shield and not deal with anything.

It broke my heart to see him isolate himself because he didn't feel like he could express his true emotions. He simply did not feel comfortable to open up and I was not sure how to gain that trust.

I knew that his own bullying behavior was not an appropriate response to his emotions but knowing some of the reasons behind his behaviors helped to understand him as a person. It was difficult to get inside his head, so it became very important to me that I was able to really hear him when he complained about not being picked for a game, pushed to the end of the line or made fun of by the kids at school. If anything, I was grateful that I was able to find sympathetic reasons for his lashing out, and that with love and time we could resolve this!

What we desperately needed was respite care. Respite care is a time when the child goes to another home for a needed break for the foster parents. We needed occasional overnight care and weekend care. We were allowed one weekend per month and ten hours per week, but I could use only licensed homes. The problem was there were no homes within twenty miles of us. Luckily, my co-teacher Sue, stepped up and had her home licensed for respite. She and her family were my saving grace. She was able to keep him whenever I needed a break and was flexible with her time. Ilyas loved her family dearly and knew he couldn't get away with acting out.

We also needed to get the rest of the family more involved. Zak was amazing to have at home and would often deflect issues before they became bigger. Biff began to take Ilyas on more outings and they did errands together and went to the arcade, park, or watched a movie. The older kids would visit from out of town and they also began to show Ilyas how much they cared for him. They would spend some one-on-one time with him and he soaked it all up greedily. While Billy was his champion, Zoe was his advocate. She had strong feelings about his place in the world and did everything she could to make sure he was given the same fair and just treatment as any other child. Even if it was just projecting her thoughts in front of him that he was a strong boy, a good boy and a deserving boy. He literally puffed up with pride when he heard those words from someone other than his parents. Bekah was the quieter, calmer side to his intensity. She remained calm when all his fury was breaking loose around us, and he could look to her for stability and support. She never wavered in her love for him and wouldn't lower herself to his level to engage with him during his outbursts.

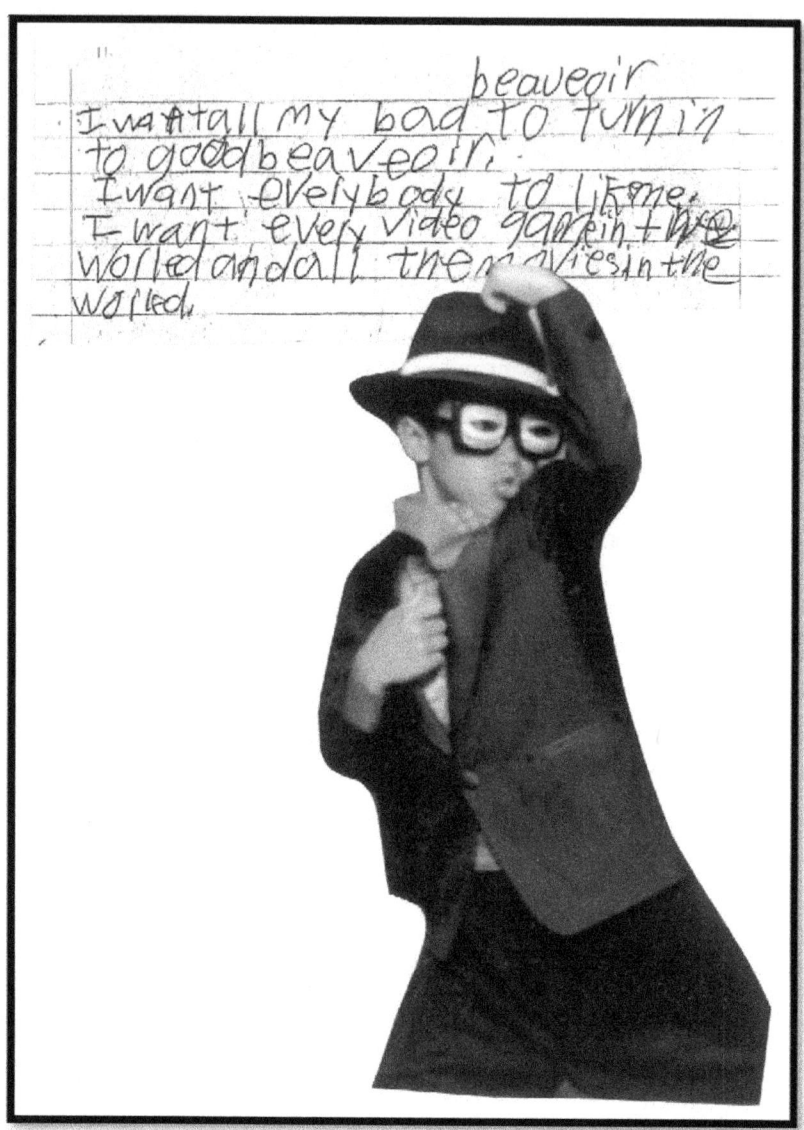

Ilyas writes about "My Perfect Day" age 8

Journal Entry #7 (March)
The Golden Rule

The Golden Rule. This is so hard for Ilyas. He really resists trying to feel empathy for others. He resists trying to put himself in someone else's shoes. As with an infant, in raising Ilyas the days are long, and the months are short. Seven months with us and we are still working on things he should have learned in kindergarten.

His teachers at school and the YMCA leaders have requested that the support counselors stop coming to school. They are not helping him. The counselors let him walk out of the classroom when he wants and play games on the playground that only two can play.

My birthday was this month. It was a Sunday and Biff had to work. Zak was at a tournament, so it was just Ilyas and me at home. It was a beautiful day, sunny and warm. A great day for the outdoors and I wanted to work in the yard and just relax. All the kids called to wish me a happy birthday, but Ilyas wouldn't even acknowledge my birthday. He was outright rude and defiant. I tried ignoring him but that made it worse. He pestered me endlessly with demands and wouldn't play on his own or help me with yard work. I really didn't want him to ruin my day for me and finally sent him to his room. Later, he wrote me a nice note all on his own!

Then it occurred to me that maybe he wasn't upset with me at all. Maybe this day just conjured up unwanted feelings. So I asked him if he was really mad at me, or was he mad at something else? He went straight to his room and wrote this note.

> Angery
> I am very with my Mom for doing bad things. She would hit me with a belt, and a hanger, and I dont go preshool, or kindgartin. But she was nice and allthorgh she did I still Love, and miss her. My dad was really bad too he was mean not caring about me.

Ilyas was suspended from school. He tried to stab a boy with a plastic fork because the kid said he was a better digger than Ilyas was. He chased him down and poked him with the fork, but it broke when he attempted to stab him. After a lecture on making different choices, I asked what he would do differently next time he was in a situation like this – he said he would bring a metal fork. UGH!

Coming up with the right consequence to fit the behavior is getting harder and harder. Writing is still the best one I have found, and he has been writing a lot. He writes definitions and sentences about actions, such as what will other people think or feel when you hurt them, call them names, take things from them and also how will they feel when you act friendly toward them or compliment them.

Apology from Ilyas

Oppositional Defiant Disorder (ODD). Add this to the list of disorders attached to Ilyas. He was a textbook case. Think of it as being opposed to new things, directions, or rules. And then oppose it—with defiance. This disorder is a given with most foster children and in fact, many children have occasional defiant tendencies. If you tell a kid with ODD not to do something, you've pretty much guaranteed the crime. Worse, if you give them too many choices or your instructions are weak or vague, you've lost them. A child with this disorder needs straight talk, strong boundaries, and clear directions. They expect the worst will always happen. They have already experienced that. To raise someone who opposes everything is exhausting.

With kids diagnosed as having ODD, arguing is useless. These children will either shut down or engage you until the argue point is completely distorted. Ilyas loved to argue and always took the negative point of view in any issue. We could be having a normal conversation (normal for an eight-year-old). As soon as the conversation got too positive, he brought out the negative side, continued to engage you and pretty soon the conversation would escalate and become heated.

When this became a pattern of debate, I tried to redirect the conversation to something more positive for him. I happened upon the perfect solution. He was an expert on and loved to talk about - The Ancient Gods. I would say "Ilyas, tell me again about the Gods. Can you start with Zeus?" And he would begin at the beginning, and tell me who married whom, which children were born and what their strengths and powers were. He could talk for an hour at a time on this topic, and it always calmed him down and centered him. This was a subject he had read about, researched, believed in, and it felt concrete to him.

After the school and YMCA both asked us to discontinue the support counselors, we asked to use them for afternoons, evenings and weekends. He was allocated twenty-five hours a week based on his support level from social services. They could take him on outings after school or weekends and help him socialize while giving us a break at home. He did not want to go with any of the counselors. He wanted to stay home and made their outings as difficult as possible.

He would yell at them, threaten to run away or refuse to get out of the car. Because of this behavior, the counselors kept changing, which in turn made Ilyas feel he had power over them.

The counselors couldn't touch or restrain him, due to their rules, and Ilyas knew he could stay an arm's length away. He would begin to make a scene and that in turn caused embarrassment and public scrutiny. He manipulated them, intimidated them.

If they would have just set strong boundaries and parameters before setting out, he would have been fine. Again, it is the straightforward talk that he responded to and if the boundaries were vague he would take full advantage. As soon as they became uncomfortable with him, they would call me or bring him home.

I was torn because he was allowed these services, but if he didn't want them it was easier and frankly less stressful to keep him with me. We asked for a few weeks without the support counselors, and they approved it for a month.

He was excited about this new development until I told him I often used the time he was gone to walk at the local state park. So now he had to come with me. He first tried all his usual tactics of complaining, dragging his feet, or acting sick, but I told him he had to come, and he couldn't bother me, as it was a time for me to clear my head. I told him he could wait on a bench and I would walk the loop, but he refused to do that. So, he trailed me, not walking with me but always had me in his line of sight. I could always see or feel him scampering behind me.

I realized that although he put up a big show of threatening to run away, he was actually afraid that I may go away. He never made good on any comments that he would leave, and always made sure he could see us. Abandonment rears its ugly head again. I wonder if that was another reason he needed us to be near him when he played. Instead of our being afraid he would take off, he was afraid we would leave him and not come back for him. He began to cooperate a little more each day as we walked, and pretty soon we both enjoyed walking together.

> **Define consequence**
> Something That happens as a result of something else, accept what happens because of one's action.

Journal Entry # 8 (April, Month 8)
Walking on Legos

This is the month that Ilyas started stealing. Big Time. It started with him taking items from home to school. The teacher notified me that he was playing with toys during class and being disruptive. I began checking his pockets and backpack in the morning and I would take away all the items he tried to leave with. He was very ingenious. He hid things in the craziest places. In the cuffs of his pants, under his armpit, in his socks or packed in his lunch. Then one day after I checked all the usual places, he was walking out the door for school. I noticed him walking funny...as if on eggshells. He almost was. He had packed little Legos into his shoes. I asked him daily, before I checked his pockets, if he was taking anything to school. I made it sound like it was a normal morning question, not a question directed toward a thief. Every morning he would say, "Of course not, Mom." And then I would find toys and think 'But of course you are.'

The big day came when he tried to take Zak's hand-held game system to school. He had put it up his pants, but when he walked out the door, trying to squeeze it between his thighs, it fell out right in front of me! Even though I took away all the items for a week, it still seemed worth his effort to keep trying. He also started bringing home items from school and the YMCA. It felt odd to pat him down when he left for school and when he came home.

Then, while we were at a volleyball game for Zak, there was a commotion in the foyer of the gym. A young boy was missing a small game for his game boy system. It had disappeared from his backpack. I knew Ilyas had to be involved in this, so I searched him. He told me he didn't take it, swore he didn't take it, looked me straight in the eye and said he didn't take it.

I was beginning to believe him and felt guilty accusing him. And then right in front of everyone, it dropped out of his shorts. He returned the game, but this was a big deal. He had to write a letter of *apology to the boy and also, he had to earn money to buy him a brand-new game. I told him he has to make this right and he has to make the situation better than before.*

He worked at chores around the house. Unpleasant chores like mucking out the goat pen and raking out the chicken coop. He also moved wood around and that took up most of his play time for a week. He did earn $30 and bought a new game which we gave to the boy.

He wrote a lot in his journal, looking up definitions of stealing and theft. We talked about the future for kids that steal. Nothing seemed to soak in until Zak came up with the idea that every time he took something he had to give something. So when he came home with a toy from the YMCA, he had to return it AND donate a toy of his own to the Goodwill. He hated the very idea of that! He hates the thought of giving up anything that belongs to him. Processions are everything to him. He stopped stealing.

Ilyas gave a boy at the YMCA a bloody nose and was sent home. He was upset because the boy, who was not part of the "Y" was using one their balls on the playground. He walked right up to him and punched him and took the ball. The kid was far bigger and older than him. He is very righteous when other people break rules, even when those are the same rules he breaks.

On one hand, it is very easy to separate myself from Ilyas. He is hard to love, difficult to like and he isn't mine. On the other hand, I see how important it is to engage and constantly reassure him we support him, whether he is good or bad. He is not a bad kid, he just makes poor choices - all the time. I see how much he honestly loves us and that makes my heart tender.

> Dear mom, I am sorry for what I said to you I hope you forgive me

"I Will" Statements

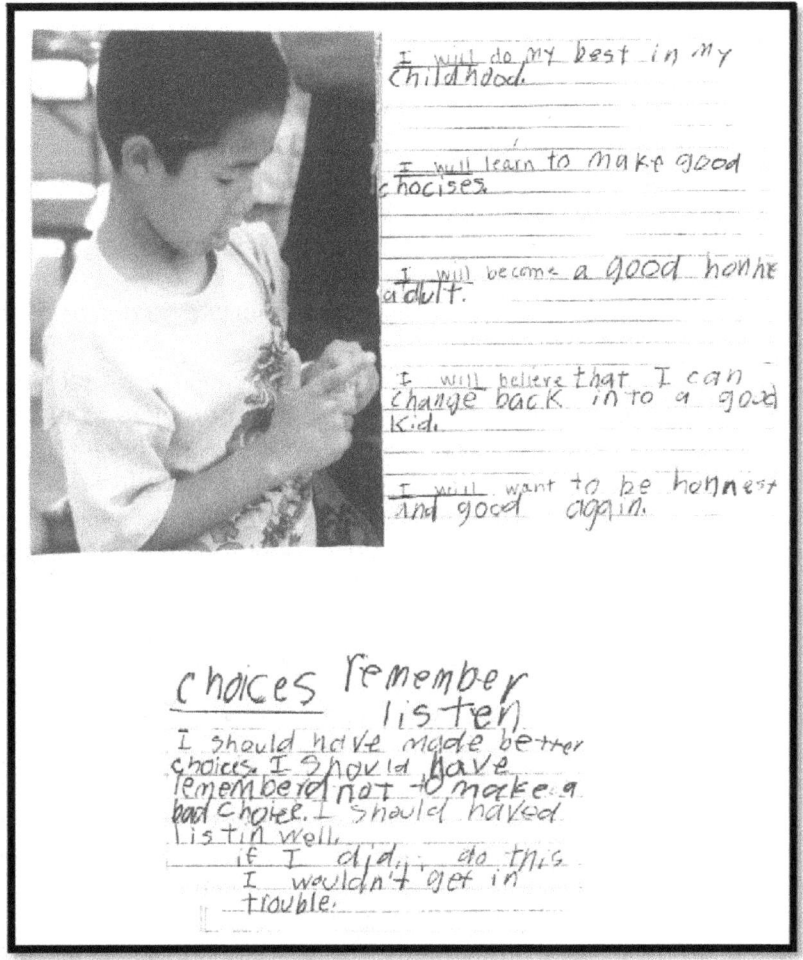

"Define - Choices"

Ilyas sees everything, every issue, every emotion. as black or white, right or wrong. I tell him to "see the gray" in life. It is possible there is a happy medium. He can't see that there could ever be a version that is murky, or muddy; only absolutes. He jumps to the conclusion that there is only one right or wrong way and nothing in between. This "all or nothing" thinking is found in depressed people all over the world. This is because it is part of the most primitive of human responses: The Fight or Flight Response. Statements like "I'm a terrible person!" or "He's perfect!" or "I'm just a failure!" oversimplify life and cause massive emotional swings. He needs to see the in-between or gray and that there is room for compromise.

How can a child diagnosed with depression and with RAD seem to attach to us so deeply? Although he didn't have the opportunity to attach to his parents, and had little capability to sort through his emotions, he was able to bond with someone. Bonding is very different from attaching. It is critical for a child with RAD to be able to bond, or he can become an adult with borderline personality disorder or even a sociopath.

Simply stated, bonding is the process of forming an attachment. Just as bonding is the term used when gluing one object to another, bonding is using emotional glue to connect with one another.

I believe Ilyas was closest to his great grandparents from the time he was very young. He bonded with them. Any pictures I have of him, came from them, and they were the only constant in his life. Though they lived five hundred miles away until he was four years old, they visited him and he occasionally visited them. When the system couldn't find a place for him, he could stay with them off and on.

Eventually, he moved to the same county as his great grandparents and he visited them more often. They were extraordinary people. Even though they were in their eighties, they did everything they could to help him.

He loved and respected them, but they were just too old to parent him full time. His great grandfather, was the family patriarch, and very traditional Chinese. He wouldn't allow any of the extended family to be burdened by the great grandson that was born under disgraceful conditions, to an absent drug mom, his granddaughter. Ilyas' great grandfather was a businessman and moved to the United States in the 1970's. Most of the extended family lived in Indonesia, including his grandparents, aunts, uncles and cousins.

When we first met Ilyas, he was staying with his great-grandparents, whom he called "Tikun and Tipau." He had been at their house for a couple of weeks, coming straight out of the mental health hospital. Teaching Ilyas about honor and respect were gifts that Tikun gave him. He took Ilyas to the library for several hours every day. This is where and when Ilyas fell in love with books. He could read at a level far beyond his age, especially considering his lack of education up to that point. His Tikun and Tipau loved him very much and believed in him. And they knew how difficult he could be. We took him back to see them for an occasional overnight. When we visited with them, we always learned more about Ilyas' life before we knew him.

Whenever we were at their house, his Tikun would speak to him in Cantonese or Mandarin. Ilyas understood him perfectly but wouldn't speak it outside of their home. He did though, listen to and respect his great-grandfather when he was with them. Tikun really wanted a permanent placement for Ilyas and visited us at our house several times. He encouraged us to keep going through the difficult behaviors and helped us believe we could do this.

Bonding with his great-grandparents enabled Ilyas to bond with others. I don't believe he ever bonded with his earlier placements, mostly because they were group homes, shelters or short-term placements.

 Abandoned children need time to believe that whoever is caring for them will remain in their lives long enough to create a bond. A child's saving grace is that if they have bonded with someone, even with a diagnosis of RAD, they can live a life with the hope of making deep connections and lasting love.

Journal Entry #9 (Month 9)
These Things I Believe

It's early May. Right now, Ilyas doesn't seem to care whom he hurts or how often. Every single day we battle about something. I try not to get drawn in, but he has a way of pushing all my buttons and I find myself engaged again. It goes back to boundaries and attention. He has come a long way, but at the same time he has worked out more sophisticated ways to invade other people's spaces.

Much of his behavior is irrational. It doesn't make sense at all! Why "flip out" over something little? Why go to such extremes to do something that he knows is wrong and he will get caught? What I have learned though, is irrational behavior cannot be met by rational consequences. Irrational or erratic behavior can't be calmed or changed by a rational conversation. Time is my friend. Disengaging is my guide. Then, maybe we can have a rational conversation.

We are now in a power struggle over food. He is choosing not to eat something we know he likes. It's crazy! He will spit food out, not chew or not swallow it. I feel like I am dealing with a two- year- old. Of course, the natural consequences are that he must leave the table. I pack up his food and he can come back and eat that food before he gets anything else. That is still engaging and giving him attention on some level.

The life lesson this month is "every time you lie, you betray trust." We need to be able to believe him, at least some of the time!

We also talk about backing off, or away from confrontations. Instead, he seems to greet them head on. Case in point; Ilyas got an in-school suspension for fighting on the bus. This is his fifth suspension this year in second grade. Because of the suspension, he had to miss the class field trip and spent the day in another classroom. He has been edgy and uncooperative. Also, sassy and disrespectful.

I am scared to have him miss his meds. Would he be even more moody or violent without them? Or are they making him act crazy . . . hmmm. On his overnight visit this month with his great grandparents, he was also rude and disrespectful. Although reluctant to stay with them very often, he has always behaved pretty well for them.

I am trying to have Ilyas write only positive definitions, or statements. "I will" statements, by virtue of those two words have to be positive. I believe, from teaching, coaching and parenting that "I will" statements to be a self-fulfilling prophecy.

He made me a Mother's Day card all by himself and went with Biff to pick out flowers for me. Very sweet and sincere.

It is late May and I just found out that Ilyas has bad dreams, nightmares, almost every night. When I asked him why he didn't come wake us up, he looked horrified. I told him we would comfort him, or he could crawl in bed with us until he felt safe. Then I realized what the horrified look was about. He had never even been inside our room. He wouldn't even walk through the door. Why?

April Martin

I asked him to write about what scares him.

> list
> **5 things that scare you**
>
> 1. One thing that scarres me is bad dreams because they make me have a bad day.
>
> 2. One thing that scare me is trying to shoot me because I will punch them.
>
> 3. I will be scared of me breakin my head because I will go to the hopital and stay in for a week.
>
> 4. I will be scared of my foal parentshiping me because it makes me afride of them.
>
> 5. I will get scaled of talken because the prinicopin it would be Embealasing.

When he showed me his writing, we sat down together to talk about what he wrote. I asked him to tell me about it. He sadly told me the dreams happen almost nightly. He won't tell me what they are about. But it is clear...

   *He is scared of violence.
   *He believes he is destined or fated to lead a life of violence and he feels powerless to change that course.
   *He is afraid of getting hurt because he is scared he will go back to the hospital (he was hospitalized for an extended amount of time in a hospital psych ward where he had no visitors except for his social worker who came once a week).
   *He is scared that his real parents will find him and take him away. He is afraid of them.

I spoke with his therapist regarding the bad dreams, and the fact that he won't come out of his room at night even when he is scared and alone. After several sessions, Ilyas began to talk about some of his past trauma and experiences. He opened up, and shared with her, stories of unspeakable abuse and molestation from the time he was very young. This abuse happened in the bedroom. Undeniable terror on his end, and fear that it could happen again, invaded his dreams at night.

This also started proceedings with CPS (Child Protection Services) into child sexual abuse that became full-fledged investigations, but to what end? These adults had already been convicted of multiple infractions; just add these to the list. What more does this little boy have inside him that he is having to deal with every day?

We ended all conversations about it for now. It was not the right time for him to continue to process this and deal with all the ramifications abuse can bring. It was time for us to care and nurture him. We had to convince him he is safe, and the abuse was not his fault and he can trust us.

With the discovery of the molestation, it brings Ilyas' abuse to all four forms of abuse in children as defined specifically by the State Statutes: sexual abuse, physical abuse, emotional abuse and neglect. It should stand to reason then, that his behavior is clearly indicative of his trauma, and is actually expected for a child with his background.

The growing understanding of early brain development, clearly shows the effect on behavior with children from abuse. According to the Triune Brain Theory, the "reptilian brain" controls our automatic physical response such as breathing, swallowing and heart rate. The "mammalian brain" is where we get our awareness, concern for others and emotions. The "neocortex" is the seat of logical process such as speaking, writing and planning. With it we can think in the abstract, problem solve and reason.

Trauma creates heightened stress receptors, which impairs the ability to think clearly and calmly. Kids who have experienced trauma or abuse are more anxious, nervous or fearful and subsequently more aggressive and defensive than other children. They have stored up threatening memories that will be permanently stored away. Because our brain never loses a single memory, children from abuse, automatically make connections from past events and apply them to their current situations.

Ilyas was so little when he came to us. Below average in height and weight, he looked unhealthy and fragile. I thought maybe it was genetics, or maybe he just didn't get enough to eat, often enough. Research shows that in a very young child, when the brain is always in stress mode, it can stunt growth and development. Children can get stuck in a terror status, and cannot regulate their breathing, heart rate and appetite. It is always in a fight or flight course.

When the brain is constantly in a fight or flight mode, adrenaline or cortisol is pumping all the time. When continually released, it can corrode areas of the brain, interfering with memory, attention and focus. Kids that are abused are hyper vigilant, and quieting the mind is nearly impossible. The nervous system of these children operates on a constant high because they are always anticipating further danger.

That being said, the brain is amazingly resilient and self-repairing. We have seen Ilyas calming down, and he has many more quiet moments when he is peaceful and content. He has begun to grow, looking healthier and happier.

Opening up to his therapist about the molestation was a huge step. It was one part of the puzzle the social workers were afraid had happened but didn't have evidence of. Now that Ilyas had talked about it, it was as though he could share the burden. He seemed relieved that the secret was out. I could see the difference in his body language. He was more relaxed and not as guarded. We promised Ilyas the abuse had nothing to do with him, and that he was not responsible for what happened to him.

Now that we understood what was going on at night with him, we could help him through his bad dreams. I couldn't imagine feeling all alone in the world with only your terrifying memories invading your sleep. He could come and wake us up and we could sit with him or let him talk about his dreams and help him process them.

With everything he has been through, it is easier to see how life is

"All About Ilyas."

Children depend on those who love them to tell them who they are. Studies have shown that a child's self-esteem is founded on the parent's beliefs and expectations. Children who are continuously "put down" or verbally abused are vulnerable to poor self-esteem and lowered confidence in themselves. Likewise, neglected children, have a greater risk of crippling their development socially, academically or otherwise. Children with a poor self-image have a much harder time learning in the classroom, at home and in social situations. They often have an inner critic that is also telling them they will fail, and they are stupid.

However, it is never too late to begin to build a child's self-worth.

We work constantly on trying to convince Ilyas that he is a smart boy who has a big heart. We try to instill in him his value and contribution to our family. It may sound contradictory with our version of tough love, because he is often dealing with the consequences of bad decisions or behavior. It could seem that we don't care for him because we make sure he follows through and is responsible for his actions. But the opposite is true. It has been proven that children feel much more secure with strong guidelines and borders. They innately understand that those restrictions are there for their safety and are put there because people love and care about them.

In studying child development, I learned that children learn by modeling and copying. They listen, observe and imitate. The most effective tool I have learned to use with all my children is projecting positive comments. I sometimes will enlist the help of another adult, but it can be done anywhere and anytime. I simply talk to someone about my child when I know they can hear but are not part of the conversation. Not hard to do with Ilyas, as he is always within earshot of all my conversations. I talk about him as if I didn't know he was there and relate an especially funny story or event where he did something positive. Or I simply talk about him and say things like how well he did at school that week, how fast he can run, or how amazing he is at math. Then without acknowledging that I knew he heard, I go on with my day. You can almost see him physically puff up with pride.

Journal Entry # 10 (June, Month 10)
Fuming and Furious

School is out! We got Ilyas' last report card and he ended the year going up in all his academic subjects and getting higher marks in work habits and citizenship.

He has been very angry with me lately. He became quite upset when I told him he couldn't go to a friend's house when we were about to leave to run errands. He flipped out and over reacted with yelling, screaming, and ranting.

Later that night I talked to him about getting angry over being disappointed. We talked for a while but then he covered his ears and started saying "la,la,la". I sent him to his room. He was so angry at me he passed these notes out under the door. It was kind of funny though because he didn't have any paper to write on so he ripped up his lunch sack and wrote on pieces of it.

A couple of days later when he was mad at me again, he stormed off to his room and slammed the door behind him. We have a big rule about slamming doors in our house, so I took his doorknob off. Now when he tries to slam his door it goes only so far and then instead closes softly with a "poof" of air. Damn, it just won't slam!

Trigger # 3 – Disappointment

His humor and quick wit is starting to come out more and more. His impressions of Yoda and Darth Vader can always get a laugh. He also has been quicker to see humor in situations and actually thought it pretty funny when his door would just "poof."

He attended a week-long YMCA sleepover camp and the rest of the family all went to Colorado to watch Zak play in his volleyball Nationals. We wanted to take some extra days to visit relatives while my coworker, Sue kept him. We got a call from the camp that they were kicking Ilyas out because he was fighting. We were so far away, and he was still raising my blood pressure! Sue was able to talk to the camp personnel and they agreed to keep him if he behaved. It was all over something trivial. Trivial to us maybe, but perception is reality. In Ilyas' reality, everything that bothers him is amplified and he acts on emotions and perceptions.

He had another meltdown after we got home and passed this note under his door.

Social services take threats like these very seriously and had to investigate exactly what Ilyas meant by this. It turns out he was just trying to get our attention and it was just that - a threat. I think he found out quickly those behaviors don't get you the kind of attention you want.

I tried to get him to turn toward a mirror when he is arguing or acting out. I want him to see his face and the attitude that is written all over him in his body language. I finally tricked him into turning around, facing a mirror mid-sentence. Yikes! He was mad at me yet shocked at the look he was projecting. Now when he rants, I hold up my hand, fingers splayed out, and say "mirror." Then he knows I am telling him his visual mannerisms need to be checked. It sort of lets me disengage and I then I often can walk away without a confrontation, knowing my message was sent. Loud and clear.

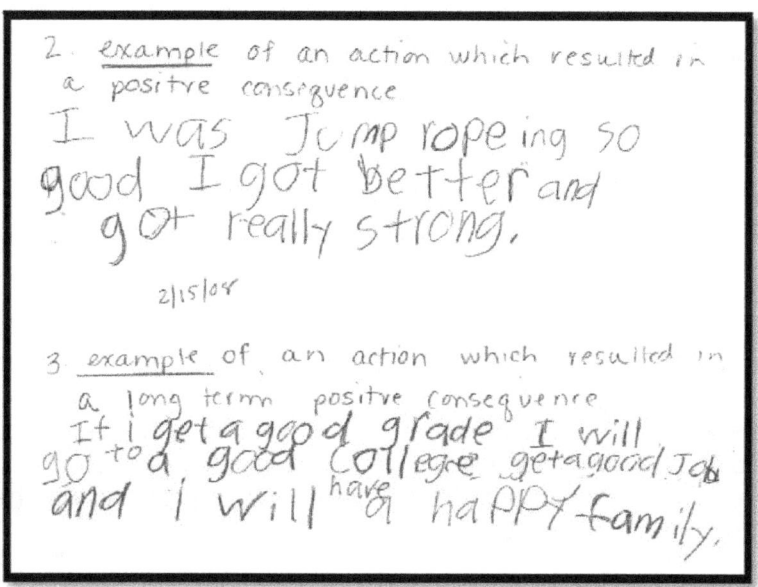

When kids believe they have value and a role in the world, it promotes self-esteem and confidence. Children need to master their environment, whatever that is at the time. It could be on the playground, learning to pump their legs on the swings, or to climb higher on the play structure. They practice, practice, practice and then one day it happens. They get it! That child is bursting with self-confidence and that feeling carries over into more difficult and risky tasks in all aspects of their lives. They simply feel good about themselves. They can go and conquer something else, be it math or friendships.

The only way that kids can accomplish this is to be able to experience skills in their environments. Often foster kids haven't had the time or place to do that. They are sometimes in the very middle of problem solving when they are moved again, either back and forth to birth parents, or foster homes.

Many kids, fostered or not, face this same issue. Children with helicopter parents or parents that hover and offer too much help, have similar problem with self-esteem. These kids get pushed on the swings way too long and don't get to learn on their own by trying over and over again. These parents are in fact telling their children that they aren't capable on their own and need help. As parents, we need to push and encourage our kids, and show them you believe in their abilities even though it may be a tough task that will take hard work to conquer.

We must prepare Ilyas to believe he is capable of making good decisions and choices as he grows up. He can do that by gaining confidence in his controlled environment now, so it won't be a harsh reality later on. He needs the chance to learn hard work and diligence to accomplish a behavior.

We pushed Ilyas to conquer his environment in a positive way. Each time he mastered something, his self-worth grew, and he felt better about being able to attempt the next thing in life.

He is starting to believe he is smart. And beginning to believe that he is a good boy, who sometimes makes bad choices, but those bad choices don't make him a bad kid. He is, in fact, a great kid who has so much to offer and contribute to the world.

Journal Entry #11 (July)
My Personal Struggle

Ilyas is having a great summer! He loves his camps and being away has made a big difference in all of our behaviors. The sleep away camps have given us a much-needed break and they have reinforced the skills we have been working on. Most of those are friendship skills and getting along with people. Being willing to give and take is so much a part of keeping friends and building trust.

He can swim like a fish now ... 40 lessons later ... and we go swimming as often as we can. He has a new support counselor that has children and should be more experienced. He takes him to the arcade and the beach boardwalk and my hope is he will be able to handle any issues that pop up when they are together.

Ilyas seems to genuinely love living here and wants to be here. He is working harder on trying to behave and follow directions. When he does melt down, he gets over it faster.

He is running around the neighborhood playing with different kids and spending a lot of time playing on his own in the backyard. He and Zak go to the creek, go on hikes, adventures, and often out for ice cream. They sometimes go skateboarding. They are definitely videogame buddies and of all of us Zak has taught him patience and sportsmanship.

He still does, of course, have issues with boundaries and when he breaks a rule, he gets very upset with me if I have to give him a consequence. His anger at something small is still way out of proportion. He goes from 0-10 instead of gradually ramping up or based on the issue at hand.

The process for him to leave our house, that we started in February, is finalizing this month. We have had him for a year, but now he will leave at the end of the month. We had a meeting at the county offices, called a TDM (Team Decision Meeting). At the meeting, there were social workers, therapists, counselors and supervisors. They have *recommended that Ilyas needs a higher level of care, and won't be placed with a family, but with a level 14 group home.*

Group homes are rated on a scale with a level 14 being the highest.

These homes are able to provide the most mental health care and counseling to their kids. It was a very intense meeting with everyone agreeing that we did the best job we could, that he has come a long way, but continues to need a lot of extra care and resources.

I went home to a little boy who now can play on his own for hours. He is content. He looks healthy and tan. He has grown taller, he has filled out and is just above average in height and weight. There is an aura of joy around him, and the darkness has faded. He still has issues, but they have dimmed with the passing of summer. He is affectionate and caring…AHHHH!

Team Decision-Making (TDM) Plan

Department of Family and Children's Service

Date: 08/11/08
Case Name: _____
Case Number: _____
Focus Children: ILYAS

Issues	Action Steps	Time Frame	Person(s) Responsible
Ilyas' acting out and oppositional behavior has led to problems at school & foster home	(1) FFA has given notice (2) ITFCS has been utilized (for has been unsuccessful)	done	April, Diane
Ilyas' emotional state and condition is due to significant abuse	(1) Has participated in counseling (2) Has received psychotropic meds	ongoing	Katherine, Diane, April, Kristen
Ilyas could benefit from a higher level of care	(1) SW will complete and submit misc. referral for level 14 care.	by wed. 8/13/08	Kristen
Significant relationships	(1) Ilyas' current caregivers wish to maintain a relationship (2) Great grandfather and GGM wish to maintain relationship	ongoing / ongoing	April's family / Kristen to arrange visit

Mother's signature: _____
Father's signature: _____
S.W. signature: _____ Signature/Relationship: Diane Hersh, MA FFA Social Worker
S.W.S. Signature: _____ Signature/Relationship: M. Mutz, Foster mom
Other S.W.: _____ RSC Signature/Relationship: _____ Support Counselor
Facilitator: _____ Signature/Relationship: _____ Therapist

Meeting Notes

Last February, we asked that Ilyas be moved to a different placement after one year. Now that timeline is coming up in a month. At the time, I felt giving them a 6-month notice was more than fair. I was ready then and there to have him removed, but I wanted him to at least finish out one full school year in the same school. We never expected we'd have a permanent foster child, and we certainly didn't enter into a fost/adopt situation purposely. We imagined kids would be coming and going all year round. But we have only ever had Ilyas, and not only has he grown attached to us, we have grown attached to him.

However, I need to keep the big picture in mind. We cannot adopt him. He has huge issues that we are not trained to deal with. He is still young enough, at age eight, to be adopted. I have had to go on blood pressure medication and the stress level is almost always high. With our youngest going to be a senior in high school, I can see the light at the end of the tunnel for school and parental obligations. Ilyas is only eight years old, And we are old enough to be his grandparents.

So it was settled. We had a date and time. His removal was sure to be emotional, so it was necessary for social services to come prepared. They scheduled therapists, counselors and social workers to meet at our home on Monday morning at 8:00 a.m.

Ilyas had no idea this was about to happen and in fact, asked us again "When will you adopt me? Please adopt me."

Journal Entry # 12 (1 year in our home)
The Decision

I realized that I had been thinking more about myself than about Ilyas. What was best for him? Certainly not a level 14 group home. I envisioned him ending up being a pawn for older boys and getting into trouble, fights and eventually drugs and alcohol. He had such a tough exterior, but he was so vulnerable and fragile underneath. I couldn't help but feel he would give up, that he would feel abandoned once again and lose hope for a normal life. I realized we were more invested in this little guy than we had imagined.

As his parents, albeit foster parents, we needed to feel good about what happened to him. We just couldn't reconcile ourselves to him leaving. Biff and I spent Sunday afternoon agonizing over the decision we had made, and what inevitably was going to happen in the morning. We had for the most part decided to make this decision on our own without input from our other kids. We were the parents after all, and this was a parental decision. Yet, we would miss him and always wonder if we had done the right thing.

We loved him.

It was Biff who ultimately made the choice for both of us. He knew in his heart that Ilyas needed us and we needed him. That was enough for me. The evening before they came to take Ilyas, we called our social worker. We told her we wanted to keep him.

Our social worker couldn't contact "the team" on Sunday, so early the next morning, counselors, social workers and therapists showed up at our house thinking they were there to facilitate the removal of Ilyas. We had sent Ilyas off with Zak. When we announced we were keeping him, there was a lot of emotion; crying, and tears, but also cheers, hope and optimism all around. It touched us to see these people, that worked with damaged kids every day, still had deep and raw feelings for every one of them.

Honestly, the emotions Biff and I felt at the time were simply, relief and joy. We had come so far in a year. We were starting to see the happy Ilyas more and the dark Ilyas less. We know it won't be easy but in my heart, I feel it is the best thing for him.

As for the kids, Zoe feels we need to finish what we started and is the most emotional, tearing up when she thinks about abandoning him. Zak looks at him like he is his little brother, very possessive, and therefore should not be going anywhere. Bekah is most worried about how keeping him will affect us, but she is supportive of our decision and thinks of ways to lighten our load. Billy, once again, sees nothing wrong with Ilyas, and has the ability to look past all flaws in all people. He is so tolerant, and feels we have no choice but to keep him.

As for Ilyas, he dodged a bullet he didn't know was heading his way. He loves our home and everything that comes with it. Here he is a part of a big family, with four siblings that all care about him. He has learned to rely on the boundaries we have set up and the rules we have established. He knows that these will be adhered to without exception. He has just begun to show respect for these rules and his freedom and understands he has a good life.

All of us make assumptions about children's behavior and developmental levels, based on age. This normally works, because for most children, development takes a normal course. Most aspects of their development match their age. For example, an average eight-year-old is physically, emotionally, intellectually, and socially at an eight-year-old level. If you look at this eight-year old's development as a puzzle, all the pieces would fit nicely together.

Children who experience abuse and neglect, will often miss milestones or exhibit delays in some parts of their development. A child from neglect won't normally develop physically or socially at the correct rate. A child who has been verbally abused will be behind emotionally. Some of their development can be on track and some behind.

Foster children especially, can be on different developmental levels at the same time. They can be physically big and emotionally a train wreck. They can be academically behind and socially ahead. They could function emotionally at their age level, but at a much younger level intellectually.

It is important for foster and adoptive parents to identify each piece of their child's puzzle, so they can better understand how their child functions. If you can understand that perhaps your child is ahead academically but behind socially and emotionally, then you can help them better balance their development. Taking away the abuse or neglect these children have experienced, only stops the abuse or neglect. It does not guarantee a child's normal development.

Research has shown that children progress through certain stages of development and no stage can be skipped. It is important that the foster family begin to care for each child at their actual age of development, and not their chronological age. This can be quite a task, especially when a child is at several different stages.

Expectations of behavior based on age are common among teachers, coaches, extended family and friends. They see an eight-year-old and expect eight-year-old behavior, but instead witness a child that can't handle disappointment, has tantrums yet could have a vocabulary well advanced for their age. How many times have we heard, "act your age." In reality, maybe they are. It can be frustrating for foster parents, trying to provide the basic needs of food and shelter, to now be called upon to diagnose stages of development. On top of that, they have to figure out how to help their child catch up in certain areas while continuing to drive to meetings and appointments, and also caring for other children and spouses.

I would put Ilyas' "puzzle" at age eight to be unworkable. Pieces would not fit together no matter how you turned them. His chronological age was eight. His social age was probably six. His emotional age was two and his life experience age was thirteen. To get him to function as a "whole eight-year-old" we needed to work on his emotional and social age. At the same time, we had to try to minimize his reliance on life experiences to get through his day.

His life experience part had seen aggression, stealing, lying and drugs. We needed to create new age-appropriate life experiences for him, so he could now draw from those. That meant including him in family events and showing him how a family can function. We made sure he felt accepted which helped him feel safe and secure.

We also needed to meet him at his younger self, emotionally and socially. For a child that is at a chronological age of two, you can expect tantrums, frustrations, and a short attention span. An eight-year-old, acting like a two-year-old has the same issues, but is not tolerated well socially. To accelerate the progress, we had to meet him at two and expect him to develop from there. Therein is another reason to provide strong boundaries and dependable consequences. Just as a two-year old need to hear "no" over and over, so did Ilyas - which is obvious so far in this journal!

Socially, Ilyas needed help with getting along with friends and learning when to back off and when to simmer down. That is a work in progress, but seemed easiest to implement during play, even within the family. We encouraged board games and cooperative play, so he could learn the give and take, the back and forth that happens naturally with friendships.

Eight-year olds have complicated relationships, and Ilyas doesn't seem capable of having a real friendship. He appears confused when friends get tired of him. We had to practice reciprocal actions. When someone was nice to him, be nice back. He had to learn that conversation involved two people, not just him. He can't seem to understand that in the world, it isn't "All About Ilyas."

Journal Entry #13 (September)
One Step Forward

Ilyas started 3rd grade this month. The school wasn't expecting him back and shuffled things around, but in general, seemed happy to see him. Ilyas never missed a beat, just jumped on the bus the first day of school. I told him this is his chance to turn over a new leaf and build a better reputation. He can come into the new school year a different kid and show the other kids he has changed. The question is; Can it last?

Zak has been busy lately. As a senior, he is playing water polo for his school team as well as a high level of volleyball for a club team. On the weekends, Ilyas is tagging along to games and tournaments and is feeling the lack of attention not only from us, but Zak too. He went around to all of Zak's team mates at a tournament and told them Zak was really mean to him and did mean things to him.

> Accuse Verb to blame and say that somebody has done something wrong
>
> I accused Zak of being mean
> I didn't honor Zak by telling everbody he was mean.
> I was not loyal to Zak.

I had to talk to him about those kind of lies and accusations. Not okay at all and that behavior is hard on all of us.

Frustrated, stressed, exhausted, disappointed, disheartened, discouraged, frazzled and drained. All words to describe how I feel right now, with the 3rd grader that lives under our roof. It feels defeating to see progress, then watch it fall apart abruptly.

This is how Ilyas attempts to handle good things in his life. Whenever he feels like the universe is in line and the world is on his side, he has to change that. Does it come from believing he doesn't deserve to be happy? I guess it is the feeling that he has lost some control and wonders how he will feel when the good goes away. He needs to brace himself for the bad. If you expect the bad, then you won't be disappointed when it comes. So, he brings on the bad in his own terms.

> I should know
> My words can hurt
> Sombody's feelings
> do not say mean things
> be nice treat
> People like you

We saw Ilyas' psychiatrist (Dr. P) once a month. We went over what was working and what was not. He involved us as foster parents in the therapy sessions and gave us time to vent or ask questions. He helped us feel we were doing as much as we could to help Ilyas. His advice was always helpful and heartfelt. It was important to feel validated in our care of this child, especially validation by an expert who saw foster kids daily. As foster parents, there was often a feeling of seclusion in parenting. The support and validation that came with an honest comment got us through the tough times.

From the first time we met Dr. P, he never tried to push Ilyas to open up. He let him play, fidget and talk about anything and everything. He patiently steered the conversations to reveal some of Ilyas' inner thoughts. I watched Dr. P with Ilyas. He would listen intently, then pause before answering, as though pondering a deep thought about what Ilyas said. He made what Ilyas said seem important. He made him feel important.

I had concerns about the counseling required for Ilyas regarding his molestation. The social workers knew how uncomfortable he was with one-on-one counseling, so they pushed him to participate in group therapy. This group therapy consisted of kids up to age eighteen that gathered to discuss and examine their personal sexual abuse experiences. It was led by a trained therapist, but I didn't want him to go. There were many inappropriate TV shows, movies and games I wouldn't let him watch because of his age. I didn't feel it was in his best interest to replay his horrible molestations and listen to those of others. Not at eight years old.

Dr. P agreed. He said Ilyas did not need to deal with or revisit his molestations at his age. He recommended that he wait until puberty or even until he was a young adult. Someday, when the time is right, Ilyas may want to talk about what happened to him. But the time was not now.

Journal Entry #14
The Quesadilla Diet

I went to "Back to School" night. Ilyas has a teacher that we are familiar with. She is firm and academic, so a good fit for him. With all the parents seated in their students half sized desks, I raised my hand. I introduced myself as Ilyas' foster mom, and a parent that was well known in the community, but not as much with this generation of parents. I explained that although he is a foster child, he lives in a stable,and loving environment. I told them he had a big heart, wants to have friends, and was turning over a new leaf this year. Last year he had a bad reputation (well deserved) and was never invited to any play dates or birthday parties. After the meeting, several parents came up to me and said their child had mentioned that Ilyas had changed a lot and was more fun to be with. We set up a few play dates and some promises to birthday parties.

We are falling into a sort of routine. Good days and bad days, but more good than bad days. He is on the swim team now and swims twice a week. He looks forward to those days and has won several ribbons at the meets. They are prized possessions. They hang in his room and he proudly shows them to everyone that comes over. At school, he has won several awards for behavior and one for being the most improved student. These awards are presented in front of the entire school at an assembly. He is also very proud of these awards. He hasn't been suspended once so far (it's just been two months) and hasn't even been benched during recess.

But the power struggles continue at home. Right now, dinners have become ridiculous. What happened to the kid that ate everything? He will take forever to finish his food, even though it was something he gladly ate a week ago. He will eat one item and leave the rest. All a fight for power. Who will win? The adult of course.

So I came up with what I call the "quesadilla diet." I asked him what I could give him that he will love and eat willingly? I told him I *felt bad, and I was tired of forcing food on him. He looked pretty smug and replied that his favorite food was a quesadilla.*

Acting like I was catering to his whim, I made him a quesadilla while serving the rest of the family something else. He ate it with a satisfied look on his face. The next morning for breakfast, I placed a quesadilla in front of him, and exclaimed how lucky he was that he got his favorite food for breakfast too. Then I told him that I had packed him one for lunch! Wasn't he the lucky boy. After school, I made him one for snack and another quesadilla for dinner, while serving a different dinner to the rest of the family. He was stumped. He knew he had to eat it, since he had made the big deal of not liking anything else, but he looked longingly at the pasta we were having.

At breakfast the next morning, he broke. He didn't want a quesadilla, he wanted pancakes like everyone else. Before we could begin a new issue over food, I had him write up an agreement that he would eat whatever food was out in front of him. We keep it posted in the kitchen.

> I argee whatever my mom puts in front of me I will eat it on time without fussing
>
> • ILYAS

Children in foster care frequently have problems in the area of eating. Children who have not been fed regularly or consistently may develop a survival mentality toward food. When children are not fed reliably, do not get enough food, or have to compete for enough, they become anxious. When food-insecure children do have access to food, they often don't trust that it is coming again in adequate amounts.

Some children approach food with a "vacuum" mentality-- that is, eat as much as you can as fast as you can! Some children have a survival mentality that makes them anxious around food. If they haven't been able to count on regularly or consistently being fed, many children will eat as much as they can when food is available. They may become anxious if they think others are getting more food than they are. Other children can't tell when they are full and may eat until they vomit.

Some children may hide or hoard food in the room. Sometimes this food isn't even edible, such as stale sandwiches or mushy, molding fruit. Hoarding food stems from emotional anxiety or want. On some level, children may feel that they can't get enough because they haven't been able to get enough. They may feel less anxious if they have stashed some food.

Ilyas hid food in his room. Under his pillow, under his bed and in his shoes in his closet. It often was food from our snack box (always open and available), but sometimes I would find a half of a sandwich or part of some fruit. I didn't really address this issue head on. When I found food or wrappers, I just cleaned them up and made sure he knew there was food available at all times. Even during the "quesadilla diet," he had access to the snack box and drinks in the refrigerator.

We continued to have food issues with Ilyas, even with him holding food in his cheeks for hours before chewing and swallowing. I just pretended that I didn't notice most of the time, and he seemed embarrassed and self-conscious of the behavior himself. I noticed he wouldn't look at me and he avoided conversation when his mouth was full, probably thinking I wouldn't notice. I mostly wanted to diffuse any more food related power struggles with him.

Journal Entry #15 (November)
Theft

Ilyas is back to stealing. He will take whatever he wants and right now he wants everything. He has been caught with stuff from school again, and also items from other people's homes. Last weekend he went to his great grandparents' house. He had $5 with him from the tooth fairy and told me he was going to ask his Tikun (great grandfather), to take him to Target to buy some Pokeman cards. When he came home, he had an awful lot of cards and also some Bakugon balls (Pokeman related toys).

Later in the week Tikun called to ask me about my giving Ilyas so much money. Ilyas had told me that he got the money from his great grandfather and told his great grandfather he got the money from me. After confronting Ilyas, I found out that he took over one hundred dollars. He said he would go up to his Tikun's room and steal money from his wallet and put it in his own wallet. He did this several times.

It stumped me as to why Ilyas felt he needed to steal money. Especially from his great-grandfather. He probably could have talked his way into buying what he wanted, yet he chose deceit over honesty. Of course, he had to write a letter of apology to his great grandfather and he had to tell him the truth about how he took it.

> I need to tell you something I stole your money Every second I could go to your room and I would go to your wallet and steal either one doller or 5 dollers or 20 dollers then I would run back to the living room and put it in my wallet and then I asked if we could go to target and you said in the afternoon and I said OK I lied about when I said I got it from parent told them I got it from you. I feel so bad I think I was really bad to do it. I am so ashamed. I will have to do 110 chores to make it right. I also have to earn back my toys and video games back I am going to learn to give and learn that giving will give me peace and joy I am sorry I am going to earn your trust back so you will believe in me again. Taking is stealing. Stealing is taking the truth away.

I also had him memorize a phrase from the book The Kite Runner *by Khaled Hosseini. This phrase had to do with theft. It explains there is only one sin and that is theft. I had him write it over and over, until he memorized it. He must have written it fifteen times this month. I am worried that if he doesn't stop this he will end up in Juvenile Hall and eventually jail he will end up in Juvenile Hall and eventually jail.*

> there is only one sin.
> only one and that is
> theft. when you kill a
> man, you steal a life.
> You steal his wifes'
> right to a husband,
> rob his child of a
> father. When you tell
> a lie you steal someones
> right to the truth
> when you cheat
> you steal the
> right to fairness.

As seems to be the pattern of behavior now, this was just the beginning of a downward spiral. He just keeps going down, down, down. He stole money from his friends at school and used to buy books from the book fair. Then he stole a book outright from the fair. He began to lie, mope and generally became a miserable kid. He wasn't fun to be with.

This is what happens when I say he sabotages himself. He was doing so well and now it has all come undone and he can't seem to stop or control his behavior. The friends he had made are all leery of him now, and he doesn't care. He has been benched at recess and had an in-school suspension.

The best way I can describe his current state of mind, is to say he got into a habit of negative behavior. You can't break a habit, but you can change it or redirect it. So, we looked for ways to make the days brighter and happier and let that become the habit. I had to recap each day with a positive thought about something good that happened to him, or he will only voice the bad things. We had to accentuate anything that could be seen as fun or pleasurable, so he could think good thoughts. After many structured and consistent days, he slowly began to pull out of his funk.

He earned back his new toys that had been taken away, by finishing 110 chores, one for each dollar he stole. He did these chores without complaining. Although they were small and quick jobs, he knew he deserved them. With the holiday season approaching, we began the lesson of "giving versus taking." He needed to feel the joy of giving. We talked about how he could help others in need and donated some of the toys he no longer played with. We also bought and wrapped new toys to donate. I told him each time he gave something, he would feel happy about helping and giving. I am not sure he really felt good about it but he did it without complaining and followed through.

I don't like the word "punishment." Punishment implies an act that is harsh and unforgiving. Punishment is imposed on a child and is focused on dealing with problems after they occur. It may stop the action but doesn't teach the child the right behaviors. Punishment prevents kids from learning to make their own decisions.

I do like the word "discipline." Discipline suggests deliberation and foresight. Discipline is a purposeful plan put in place before an action. It fosters self-control and self-responsibility. Discipline encourages children to be capable and responsible. Consequences are a direct result of an action. If an action is inappropriate, then the consequence should be one that instills a reminder to not repeat the action. Discipline is always about shaping behaviors. Discipline is more effective than punishment as a teaching tool.

With that in mind, using the same consequence regardless of the action, falls short of making an impact. If a parent always gives their child a "time-out" for hitting, biting, lying, stealing and so on, then that consequence loses its effectiveness. Some parents yell or raise their voice at their child for everything from not cleaning their rooms, to swearing or not finishing their homework. Then yelling falls on deaf ears because the child just ends up hearing "bla,bla,bla."

Foster children have generally experienced many forms of punishment and not as much discipline. Often, they have been physically beaten, berated, or had food or shelter, withheld by their birth parents. At many foster or group homes, the punishment is often the taking away of privileges or possessions. And it begins the minute they enter a new home. It can seem to a foster child that they have to earn a normal life, instead of being able to expect a normal life, which is a right for every child. Discipline for a foster child is simply learning the rules of the house (which should be the same for everyone) and gives the child a chance to comply.

A far more effective way to discipline is to try to make the "punishment" fit the crime. That takes creativity and thoughtfulness, but really is more fun for all involved. "Time outs," or being sent to their rooms, are valuable when a child needs a break, or before they escalate the behavior and get deeper in trouble.

If a young child hits, an effective consequence is to have them sit with their hands in their pockets. It helps remind them that hands are not for hitting. If a child needs to really understand what they did wrong, then a lecture may be called for, but that should come after the child has calmed down and not in place of discipline. Lectures by themselves are ineffective as a punishment.

Remembering that irrational behavior does not respond to rational talk or discipline, it is helpful to have some arbitrary consequences up your sleeve that you can use for indiscriminate offenses. For instance, a child could be having a bad day; arguing, talking back or antagonizing their siblings. Rather than relying on yelling, lecturing or sending them to their room, have them sharpen all those random pencils that are in the junk drawer. Or clean the crumbs from the silverware tray that are always there. They could make a list of the trees and plants on your property or draw a map of your town. It helps diffuse the situation, redirects the child and this in turn calms them down.

Working to diffuse situations before they escalate takes more effort on the part of the parent because you have to be vigilant in observing or "reading" your child's mood or behavior. Maybe your child comes home from school, slams the door, shouts at their siblings and then mopes on the couch. Instead of reacting to their action (which is a reaction in itself), give them some space and see if they can compose themselves. It could be they are merely hungry, or maybe had a rough day at school or with peers. By allowing them space, you are giving them time to regroup.

When a person takes out their frustration on someone or something that had nothing to do with the reason they are upset, it is called displacement of anger. Foster kids are often the brunt of a parent's anger, merely because they are there. They in turn go and take out their frustration or disappointment on someone or something else. If we as parents can allow the time involved to listen to each child when they are upset, then we can help them come up with a better way to handle frustrating situations. As children learn appropriate ways to handle issues and problems, then we can be instrumental in changing a lifelong behavior and break the cycle.

With Ilyas, we used the phrase "turn it around". That meant he needed to change his attitude before it escalated. At first, he couldn't do that easily, but with practice he could "turn around" his attitude fairly quickly.

When I had Ilyas write apology letters to everyone whose feelings he hurt or for items he took, I was hoping he would learn that the action was not worth the consequence. It is hard to apologize for behavior, and Ilyas had to swallow his pride when he delivered each letter he wrote. In looking up definitions, I hoped he would learn that the meaning of the word related to all people, and not just how he chose to interpret them.

Writing the *Kite Runner* phrase over and over really seemed to sink in with him. He understood that stealing was a big deal and you stole not only when you took things, but also when you lied, and cheated. Maybe it was the fact that he was tired of writing, but he stopped stealing, and at least for now that issue has seemed to have gone away.

> there is only one sin. Only one and that is theft. When you kill a man, you steal a life. You steal his wifes' right to a husband, rob his child of a father. When you tell a lie you steal some one's right to the truth. When you cheat you steal the right to fairness.

Journal Entry #16 (December)
Being Nine

Another birthday! Ilyas is nine this month. When I think how far he has come and how many obstacles he has overcome, I am glad we are able to make him happy.

On the other hand, he is still moody, devious and temperamental. He is dramatic. He is controlling and demanding at his worst and sweet and helpful at his best. His "poor me" attitude doesn't garner much attention and Zak is famous for telling him we won't be throwing him a pity party anytime soon. He'll ask Ilyas, "Do you want cheese with your whine, or balloons for your pity party?" That makes Ilyas mad, but at the same time he laughs and lets it go. He's getting over things quicker and doesn't hold on to the negative as long as he used to.

This month at school, they did eye exams. I got a call from the school nurse saying she was worried about Ilyas' eyesight. I sighed and waited for the explanation. She said that he told her he couldn't read or even see the chart. Then, he asked her to turn it upside down. Voila! He could read it perfectly. Of course, this concerned her. I laughed at first, but then felt bad, because she sounded honestly worried. I told her I would have him examined. When I asked him about it later, he said he didn't want to have his eyes checked at school. So first he acted like he couldn't see, but then decided to try it upside down for fun. Trickster!

Master manipulator. He could manipulate doctors, teachers, workers - anyone! It reminds me of the day he told his YMCA that it was his last day. He said his parents needed a break and he was moving. They quickly pulled together a party, took pictures and were upset at the sudden change. When he showed up the next day, the "Y" called me. I knew nothing about it, of course. Another day after an especially exasperating afternoon, we went out to dinner. He convinced the waiter that I hadn't fed him all day, and he was starving. The waiter kept eyeing us like he wasn't sure if he should confront us or not.

Another time he convinced a substitute teacher that he was blind in his right eye and couldn't take the test. I almost always ended up amused. He was so smart and had the ability to figure out an advantage in every situation. Most of the time these situations turned out to be comical but other times it left people upset and frustrated with his antics. If he caught a weakness in someone he would capitalize on it immediately.

We are continuing with the theme of giving-versus-taking, especially meaningful during the Christmas season. We picked two names of needy kids off a "tree" at the post office to buy gifts for. We bought, wrapped and delivered the toys for the kids, a boy and a girl. Ilyas did a good job of at least pretending to be happily involved.

For Christmas, Bekah and Zoe donated twenty dollars in his name to the World Food Program. He was a bit taken aback, but gracious (gracious? first time), and hung the certificate in his room next to his ribbons and awards. They also got him toys and along with all the other gifts he received from the family, he was quite happy.

All the kids came home for Christmas and we had a great time hiking, playing, eating and hanging out together. Except for a few days at his great grandparents, he stayed home with the gang. When he asks why he can't do some things with all of us, I tell him it is because we cannot trust his behavior all the time. He needs to be predictable and he just isn't there yet. His main trigger is disappointment, and you never know when that will rear its ugly head. It could be over being told to take a shower or waiting for his turn.

It is important for us to remember that Christmas presents and the giving and receiving of them cannot be based on behavior alone. He is a nine-year-old boy that deserves what every nine-year-old boy wishes for at Christmas. That is a magical morning with gifts he never even knew he wanted, waiting for him under the tree. And that is what we gave him.

Ilyas originally came to us with an old suitcase packed with a few clothes that were mostly too small or outdated. Most foster kids travel from place to place with all their belongings in a garbage bag. They don't have many possessions. Possessions are rewards usually earned, and these kids typically spend more time losing privileges than earning them. Their rooms are often devoid of personality or personal things. Just a bed, dresser and desk. I feel this is the biggest error in the process of learning to be a foster parent. The system encourages parents not to give their foster kids things they may get attached to. The reasoning is they can't take it with them when they have to pack hurriedly to go to a new home.

Think of it from a child's point of view. To never have items of their own that they can take pride in, and may certainly cherish, would be just another blow to their self-image and esteem. They can feel they are undeserving and that is why they have few possessions.

We went into foster parenting wanting to continue to parent and felt it was important to parent any child the same way we did our own kids. I made a point of putting up pictures of him or pictures he made on the wall. I wanted him to have visual reminders of who he was and how he was important to us. Like any child of ours.

The foster system issues families gift cards and a "clothing allowance". It is not nearly enough to cover clothes, shoes and accessories. The clothes and shoes that are affordable often do not hold up well, nor is there more money when they do wear out or kids outgrow them.

It is hard enough to be a foster child, but when they are dressed in used shoes, outdated clothes and too big, or too small jackets, it makes them stand out even more. What about the phrase "You look like an orphan" often used when children dress themselves. Even though it's just a figure of speech, it bears truth. It causes anxiety for a child to feel as though they don't fit in because of what they are wearing. It can feel like other kids, even adults, label them as foster kids because of their old or ill-fitting clothing. Add this to their many other angsts, and I feel like this is one that we, as foster parents, can help avoid.

Bear in mind, our desire was to raise a foster child with the same advantages of our own children. I tried to buy current styles (not name brands necessarily) of clothes and in his size. I clearly remember the first time I bought him Nike shoes. He was beyond excited, and so proud. Ilyas also did wear hand me downs from Zak and friends, but they fit him and were approved by him. A child that is dressed well goes a long way in affecting others' first impressions, and he needed all the help he could get.

Social services cautioned us about spending extra money on clothing and shoes. They were always thinking about the next placement, where he might go back to whatever clothes and sizes were available. But in my mind, it was more important, to make sure this child felt like he fit in. Only then, would he feel like he could grow and change. He had to feel proud of his appearance; then he could feel proud of his actions.

Around this time, a neighbor was giving away an iguana with all the accessories included. Ilyas wanted him so badly. I said it was okay if he would care for it. He did a good job of feeding, cleaning the cage, and playing with him. But again, social services frowned on him having a pet. What if he got attached to it and then his placement changed? I wondered, what happens when these kids are yanked away from everything they are attached to, including siblings, parents and homes? To me it seems the chance to care for something besides yourself, even for a brief time, is more beneficial than having nothing. All kids learn from caring for a pet and I wouldn't want to deny any child that opportunity.

Social services were supportive in the end. It is their job to keep an eye on situations that could be detrimental to the child. They ultimately are looking for families that are loving and stable and they will support them. I found that it was okay to deviate from the norm if you have good reasons to back it up.

Journal Entry # 17 (January, 17 months)
"No Future For You"

Third grade. This is a very important grade in elementary school. Kids begin to understand that they are part of a school system that goes on for a very long time. Homework becomes a reality and they are role models for the younger grades.

At the beginning of the year, Ilyas' teacher worked hard with him. She seemed to favor him and allowed him some extra privileges. I got the feeling she thought she would be part of the big turnaround in his life... that she could change him and make him successful. She would be that teacher that transformed him. Well, change comes slowly, and it wasn't long before Ilyas wore her out. That is what he does to people. He pushes and pushes and then shuts down without any apparent reason. He doesn't respond to generosity or kindness and pretty soon they are worn out - done - with him.

Not many people are willing to work through Ilyas' negativity, moodiness or his acting-out, even when they understand the source of his issues. So now this, his ability to wear others out, has happened at school. His teacher is no longer willing to be patient and in fact has been the opposite. She is intolerant of his antics, exasperated with his behavior and blames him for things he hasn't done. Why does he have this effect on people? They totally turn on him. I think it is often his lack of response or appreciation to others that makes people quit on him.

His teacher called a meeting with us. Ilyas and I both went. I wasn't prepared for what was coming. She sat us down and then addressed only Ilyas. She told him he was smart, but it didn't matter because he was never going to amount to anything. He didn't work to his potential. He was lazy and didn't try hard. He wasn't going to have a future. Because he messed around, he wouldn't get into college or have a successful career. She really came on strong and it was personal. I was taken by surprise and didn't know what to say. As what happens sometimes when you are blindsided, I froze. I watched as he crumbled. He was devastated.

Later that evening I wrote her an email telling her that what she told Ilyas was hurtful, and more importantly, harmful. Basically, she had told him what he already believed. He felt he was worthless and would never go anywhere in life. He knew he would never amount to anything.

She responded to my email and said she didn't mean any harm by it. She meant it as a wakeup call, so he might think about his future. She thought the tone and seriousness of her conversation would make him change his approach to school. He was only nine years old. Unfortunately, you cannot approach a child so young and so vulnerable and fragile with a "reality check." She agreed to talk with Ilyas. She attempted to explain what she meant by her lecture, but he didn't buy it. He remained completely closed off to her for the remainder of the year. As his teacher, he needed to trust that she believed in him, even when he messed up. And now he knew the truth. She didn't. So who else didn't?

It's hard to see a child crushed and fragmented so easily from comments. Because the comments said to him were by his teacher, he believed them. We have been working so hard to build his confidence. Watching Ilyas react to her remarks, reminds me how easy it is for kids to believe negative dialogue, especially about themselves.

A child with a poor self-image can hear ten positive statements about his behavior, yet one or two negative comments erases them all. The positive and negative comments should be able to equal out. Not with words. Words can cut deep and do more damage to a child's self-esteem than most of us realize. Ten positive comments minus two negative ones, equals zero. And that is where their self-worth stays, until it can be slowly built up.

Most foster kids feel they have few good or redeeming qualities. They have often been repeatedly told they are bad, worthless, and insignificant. They regularly blame themselves for the reasons they are in foster care in the first place. If they had been a cuter baby, or a smarter child, their parents would have chosen them instead of drugs or crime. "My mother would have wanted me if I hadn't cried so much." Or, "I wish I had cleaned up more, because then my parents would have loved me." If they were worthwhile, their parents would have kept them safe.

Foster kids are especially vulnerable to criticisms and judgments. Even though they appear to be tough, they have very thin protective shields that can be penetrated easily. When they have to be disciplined, which frankly can be often, they most importantly need to believe they are still valued as a person. If they feel respected by their caregivers, teachers and coaches, they can accept consequences without damaging their self-esteem.

Along with the attachment and bonding issues many foster children have, they also have missed out on the expectations and certainty that someone believed in them.

Expectations imply confidence. If you expect certain behaviors from your children, you are letting them know you have confidence they can achieve these goals. As a parent, I expect respect. I expect consideration. That expectation equals a result. Confidence building 101. They believe you believe in them.

Journal Entry #18 (February)
"You Are My Strong Man"

We signed him up for a rec basketball league and Ilyas discovered basketball is amazing! He is learning to play this game pretty well. He is one of the smallest kids in the 3rd/4th grade league, but he is hanging with the best of them. On the court, he plays like a pit bull on defense. He has amazingly quick feet and sticks to his player until they lose the ball. He is still learning how to be a team player and be a good sport, but on the court, he is great. He gets knocked down and jumps right back up and keeps going. He doesn't get angry or mad. Which is surprising.

One time his coach called out to him during a game, when it looked like he was getting frustrated. She yelled, "You are my strong man!" He heard that. And that is all it took for him to change his attitude. He beamed at her, and held himself a little higher, like he believed her. He tried so hard to please her after that. He played harder than ever.

I found an emotion in me that I didn't know was there with this little guy. One time during a game, a bigger kid threw him hard to the floor and I felt a panic, a concern, compassion and love for him at that moment. I wanted to throttle that big kid and felt so protective of mine. This is a feeling I have felt many times as the mother of our four other children, but this was the first time I felt SO maternal toward this kid.

Ilyas worked so hard to push us away and was so much work and heartache. It was really then and there I knew we were in this for the long haul - that I could never give him up to just anyone's care or lack thereof.

For foster kids, the lack of confidence manifests itself differently from other kids. They show it differently. They become toughened, and inflexible. They need to control their world. They seem arrogant, selfish and unappreciative. They are surviving.

When his teacher told Ilyas he wouldn't amount to anything, he believed her. It was easy for him to accept what she told him, because no one had convinced him he could ever be anything. Though we tried daily to instill confidence in him, those first seven years of his life took a toll on his self-worth.

Just as he believed his teacher when she told him he didn't have a future, he also believed his basketball coach when she told him he was her strong man. We could see it in his face and his body language out on the court. He broke into a huge grin, calmed down, flexed his muscles and then worked hard to live up to her expectation. She took care throughout the season, to continually point out his strengths and always made a point of making him feel important and valued. Positive comments that are sincere along with high expectations play a huge role in helping these damaged kids recover and feel good about themselves.

In order to help build up Ilyas' self-esteem, I asked him to write about what he is good at. On his own, he added a list of what he is working on.

> 5 things I'm good at -
> Video games
> Sleeping
> Sports
> Playing
> Math
>
> 5 things I'm working on -
> bieng nice
> eating without fussing
> doing theirpt
> multipication
> not bieng madso easily

Journal Entry #19 (18 months at our home)
A Normal Kid

Ilyas doesn't like to think of himself as a foster kid and continues to ask us about adopting him. He has been using our last name for some time and I haven't had the heart to deny him. His legal name appears on documents but for all his school work and sports, he uses our last name. I know this is his way of fitting in here at home, and also out in the community. He wants so much to be a part of our family.

Bekah spent a week at our house with Zak and Ilyas, while Biff and I went to watch Zoe play volleyball in college. Everything went well, though Bekah (being a social worker), observed that Ilyas' support counselors were not a good fit for him anymore. She was right.

He was getting in trouble in school again and his poor attitude was spilling over to the after-school YMCA. He was asked to leave early several times. He was giving the support counselors a hard time as well and between everyone, he had to write letters of apology almost daily. At school in general, there were daily confrontations between Ilyas and peers, the yard duty, and his teacher.

We called a family meeting. Ilyas was spiraling down again and I didn't want it to reach the lowest point. We sat down and asked Ilyas what he wanted out of life, school and family. We really wanted him to feel like he had some power here. He needed to help us help him by telling us what he wanted his life to look like. Where did he want his life to go? What did he need from us to progress in his life and in the family? We couldn't keep going on this way and he knew it.

He sat for a while, then thoughtfully and eloquently, he told us, "I want to be normal. I want to be treated like a normal kid, not a foster kid. I don't want all these people in my life, invading me, coming to my school and making me stick out, so that everyone knows I'm a foster kid.

I don't want any more counselors, therapists or psychiatrists. I just want to be a normal kid."

Wow! That seemed so real and so obvious. I felt like I had missed this part of the puzzle, and that a lot of his acting out was because of the frustration he felt about being a foster kid. He felt he stuck out like a sore thumb. I knew the services he received through the system were meant to help him, but he wasn't being helped. He was so resistant to anyone he thought was a counselor or therapist, that he refused to listen to them or let them help him.

We agreed as a family that we would all work toward his goal of being a normal kid. We would make sure we treated him normally. I told him I would try to work on what we can do about the outside support services, though I warned him that it may not be easy to change.

He also told us he really disliked his name. It was hard to understand, to spell and pronounce. He loved his nickname "S" but asked if he could officially use our last name too. We explained that a name comes with expectations. If he used our last name, then he had to hold up a reputation that had been built by our other four kids and ourselves in the community. He had to wear our name with pride.

The support counselors coming in to help us weren't working out, and we all needed a change. Ilyas had made it clear he wouldn't cooperate. They were struggling with Ilyas' behavior while trying their best to befriend him. He's a difficult case and the staff kept changing in order to try to find a good fit. While I understand their frustrations, it was hard to listen to the constant complaints in emails and phone calls. I would have liked them to deal with Ilyas and not allow him to manipulate them. They needed to be firmer, and to stop trying to process his feelings and analyze his behavior.

I felt torn between understanding their complaints yet feeling defensive because of all the criticisms about what a terror my child was. Plain and simple, he wasn't acting out because he had issues that could be helped by talking about feelings and emotions.

It's "All About Ilyas" again!

Keeping up with, and interacting with the support counselors, on top of Ilyas' behavior, was causing me a lot of stress. I didn't want to appear ungrateful nor unappreciative, because I needed their support, yet the current situation needed to undergo some changes. Based on Ilyas' behavior, I could only guess he really meant he was tired of dealing with them.

We were able to work out an arrangement that allowed us, as foster parents, to help manage the funds that were set aside for Ilyas and his level of care. He was listed at the top tier for receiving services and, as such, the state allocated extra money for his therapy and support benefits. It was enough money that they were able to fund a psychiatrist, a therapist, plus a support counselor, for up to twenty-five hours per week. His psychiatrist and therapist continued to be court mandated, but we asked to eliminate the support counselor. The money allocated for that, was now available to us for other uses. This was called ITFCS (Intensive Treatment Foster Care System) aka "In Lieu", money earmarked just for his level of care. If Ilyas wanted to be a normal kid, I knew I could spend that money in a much more effective way to help him progress toward that goal.

We signed him up for sports camps on weekends and holidays. He attended volleyball, basketball, and baseball camps. Although focused on physical skills and learning the game, the coaches incorporated social skills, sportsmanship and patience.

At these various camps, Ilyas found a place he could go where he knew no one and no one knew him, or his past. It was refreshing. He began anew and chose his own path. He loved every minute, every sport and respected his coaches. He was singled out several times as a great listener and focused camper.

Ilyas was working especially hard at learning so many new things. Proud of himself, he realized he is fast and coordinated, and felt a deeper connection to our active and sports-minded family. We were all proud of his efforts and enthusiasm.

We found a teenager who gave him private basketball lessons. We had a neighbor come and help him with his homework. He loved being on a basketball team, and did so well, so we signed him up for Little League and bought him his first mitt, bat and cleats.

Less counseling and more activity was vital in helping Ilyas obtain his goal of being a normal kid. He was a nine-year-old yet had been expected to participate in so much counseling. A nine-year-old child needs to be active and engaged and playing. He didn't want to talk about his past and think about his issues. Those issues were painful, and pain turns into frustration and anger, and acting out.

Change began to take place. Slowly. He complained less and seemed less needy. He could go a couple of days in between outbursts or tantrums. He continued to go to the YMCA after school, and then, was so busy with practices, games, and activities that he was worn out by dinnertime. A good worn out.

We were lucky to be able to work out such a deal with the foster system. Or were we? I thought we were bound to the usual benefits of his allocation of funds as mandated by the system. That we had to use the services provided and required. To be able to have input on how best to help our foster son, and how to use the money designated for him, felt like a win-win combination.

It could simply be that most foster parents don't question the usual path to getting the help their children need. But, that path must be challenged if it isn't helping the child. There are so many ways to bring out the good in children, even those damaged by trauma. It can be music, art, drama, or in Ilyas' case, sports and books. Counselors can accomplish only so much until they become another pawn in the system, in the eyes of these children.

These kids are overloaded with appointments and therapies. They know their peers are not getting daily, weekly or even monthly therapy. Activities that are geared to their particular interests may spark a child to invest in themselves, more than simply talking about it.

Journal Entry #20
Dazed and Confused

Oh My God! This morning I had Ilyas' pills in one hand and my orange juice in the other. Without looking or thinking, I swallowed his pills. I didn't realize it until later when I went to give him his pills and mine were on the counter, not his. I was horrified. For a moment I panicked, then I thought, it can't be that bad. After all, he is a small child and I am more than double his weight. His dosage was for a small child, who weighed just 50 pounds.

I forgot all about it and went about my morning routine. Then, around mid-morning I remembered about the pills. I remembered because I felt like I was in some alternate universe. One where you are groggy, yet functional. Where everyone speaks as though they are underwater, and the pace is slow motion. I walked around all day like a zombie. I didn't feel. No emotion. I didn't really care about what was happening. I felt numb. Right after I had a conversation with someone, I couldn't recall what was important about it.

Is this what Ilyas feels every day? Is this why he doesn't care? Is this the way he sees the world, school, friends on a daily basis?

What if this was my new normal? I wouldn't be fully functional at all. I would not finish tasks and I wouldn't care. I am finally truly walking in Ilyas shoes and they don't fit, they don't feel right.

Ilyas took 100 mg of Seroquel (used to treat schizophrenia in adults and children who are at least 13 years old and to treat bipolar disorder in adults and children who are at least 10 years old) in the morning and another 100 mg at night. He took 10 mg of Lexapro (used to treat anxiety in adults and also treats major depressive disorder in adults and adolescents who are at least 12 years old) in the morning. He also took 28 mg of Straterra (used to treat attention deficit hyperactivity disorder- ADHD) daily.

I knew that Ilyas had been prescribed these drugs when he was sent to the psych hospital, but why these drugs? His foster parents at the time called 911 and reported him as a "5150." This is a code used by law enforcement and psychiatrists. "5150 - When a person, as a result of a mental health disorder, is a danger to others, or to himself or herself." The police report states that Ilyas told his fost-adopt mother that he was going to stab her with a knife, and then kill himself.

The medicines that Ilyas was on, were meant to slow him down, to keep him from being depressed, and to even out his moods. No wonder he couldn't take accountability for his actions. No wonder he didn't show empathy easily and rarely cried. The drugs are supposed to have a numbing effect on a person. A kid like Ilyas who is full of life and emotions, must constantly battle against the artificial blanket that the pills provide.

After inadvertently taking Ilyas' meds and experiencing the effects of them, I immediately made an appointment with his psychiatrist. I had been so leery about taking him off the drugs because I thought his behavior would worsen. We'd been warned by social services to never miss a dose. All along, Biff suspected the drugs were keeping him from really feeling, really experiencing emotions. Now I had to agree, after my mistaken pill-popping experience.

His psychiatrist, Dr. P, promptly reduced his prescriptions steadily, and within two weeks he was off both his psychotropic drugs. We were able to reduce his ADHD medicine to a lower dose as well. It was scary at first, waiting for him to react or act out, but that didn't happen. He was fine, and slowly came alive. Every day he seemed more aware and awake. He solved problems quicker and more effectively. He seemed to be less tired and certainly less drowsy.

All along we'd assumed the drugs were supposed to help control and regulate Ilyas' behavior. After taking him off the meds, we realized they were merely drugs to put him in a dazed state. They kept him from feeling, from caring. Ilyas needed to feel! He wanted to care! His behavior didn't change, but the rest of him blossomed.

The State of California has now passed the toughest foster care law pertaining to the prescribing of drugs in the nation. Ilyas was given his in 2007, when the overuse of these medications was becoming common and often prescribed without merit or follow up.

Ilyas' file states he was severely depressed and showed manic tendencies. I'm sure he was depressed. His situation and life at seven years old, was out of his control. He had just failed another fost-adopt placement and his parents and relatives had failed him. The system had failed him.

All About Ilyas

Being held on a "5150" means a 72-hour mental health evaluation period is required. Ilyas, seven years old, was held for over two weeks. I can't imagine the feeling of loneliness, panic and terror he must have felt. His only visitor was his social worker and she could only manage to visit him twice. He was so little and had no resources to draw upon. Ilyas wasn't and isn't a resilient child. However, he is a survivor, and he will survive on his own terms in his own way.

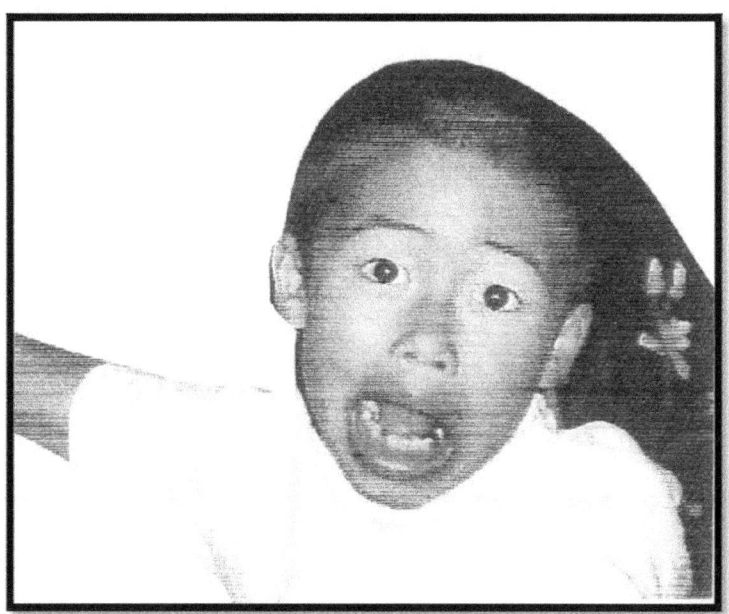

Journal Entry #21
A Capacity For Emotion

The other night we were listening to a Jason Mraz song about the loss of innocence of a child. The lyrics were about a child whose parents partied all the time and forgot about him. Forgot that he was important. The song made Ilyas cry. He said that was how it was for him. Drugs were more important than he was to his parents.

Crying over a song was new. I believe it is because he is off the drugs. He is feeling more emotions. He rarely cried, even at times he should have. He is beginning to see himself a little differently. He is beginning to put himself in other people's shoes. He is feeling empathy for the first time since we've known him.

Zak has become his new unofficial support counselor. They spend a lot of time hiking, going to the beach, exploring and taking pictures. They play video games and board games. Ilyas loves Zak more than anything in the world! He respects him and his quiet nature and doesn't act up when they are together.

> the water ballon flys thragh the air
> The sun is bright. I'm looking straight up trying to catch sight of a speck of red while running around. I see it now. Splash. it breaks against my arms. I see the remains of the water ballon on the grass. I finally relize it's impossible to catch a ballon that is being launched at you. But Zak falls down laghing.

A story about Zak by Ilyas

We used some of the funding with our new "in lieu" services for books. For the first time Ilyas really began to read for pleasure. He had always been an avid reader, but he read mostly to escape, or avoid issues. Now we were able to invest in books that he read over and over. He read and read. He carried a book with him wherever he went. These were books he picked out. He began to read book series that were far advanced for his age group.

Ilyas is into tetherball and has become the tetherball king at school. He played so much his knuckles were getting raw. I bought him a pair of bicycle gloves; the kind where the fingers showed through. He wore those gloves all day every day. Soon though, the gloves gave him a sense of power. Power like a superhero. He felt invincible. As long as he had the gloves on, he could talk back, pick fights and refuse to cooperate. He became bossy and demanding - more than usual. Away went the gloves. And he returned to his normal self. Ugh!!

I see a light that hasn't burned before. He is brighter. If he catches me noticing, he pretends to "go dark," but it is a slightly less shade of dark than before. It is clear to me, at these times, that he is controlling his emotions rather than being out of control and escalating. He is choosing to change from happy to angry, but I don't let him know I know this, because that would diminish the control he is trying to hold onto.

On Mother's Day Ilyas was very excited. He picked out his own card and with Biff's help, bought me flowers. He was so proud and excited that it made it fun to watch him. Beside himself, he couldn't wait to give me his card and flowers. We had a nice day with a hike and picnic. No melt-downs the entire day.

We love him, but he is often bigger than life. The arguing, the back and forth and picking of battles is tiring.

Ilyas feeling empathy, or at least demonstrating empathy was new. Empathy is when you can understand what others are feeling or thinking. It is the ability to put yourself in another person's situation. Kids who show empathy can imagine what kind of action or response might help a person feel better. Empathetic children understand that other people may have different feelings and perspective from their own.

Physical punishment, threats, and scolding may interfere with the child's developing ability to empathize. Foster kids often don't show empathy because they are focusing entirely on themselves. Again, survival. When children have a warm, loving relationship with their caregivers, they feel secure, and that security frees them to think about others. When they don't feel secure, they think only about themselves.

Many child development experts believe that empathy is a moral development. That is, the ability to empathize is beneficial to the species. As human beings, we are as likely to develop empathy as we are to develop language.

But what happens when surviving or looking out for yourself interferes with the development of empathy? Luckily, empathy can be learned or taught. Talking about others' feelings and reading stories about emotions and awareness are two ways to teach empathy. Be a role model. Use "I" messages to validate your child's difficult emotions.

Say to them, "I see you are frustrated, or I hear by your voice you are upset." Kids that feel secure will pick up on these cues and start responding.

Picking up on social cues is not only an important part of gaining empathy, but also in obtaining information about how you fit into the world. Social cues are the signals people send through body language and expressions. Many kids with social skill issues have trouble picking up on these cues. When kids miss recognizing these clues to what a person is thinking or feeling, they can misunderstand people and situations.

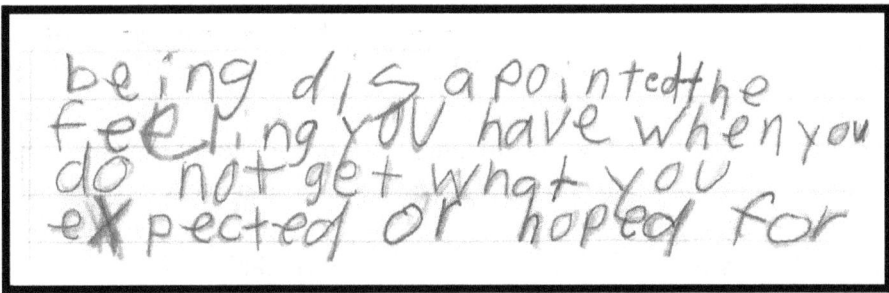

There are four main social cues - facial expression, body language, voice pitch or tone and personal space. Ilyas, like many foster kids, had not developed social skills to the point where he could understand these cues.

However, Ilyas certainly can manipulate people, which does require a certain amount of social awareness. He can also turn on his charm, with his winning smile and puppy dog eyes. Yet he doesn't pick up cues when someone is upset with him, based on their facial expression or body language, and continues to push buttons and go too far. Talking about it later, he claims he didn't realize they were upset with him, or he would have stopped.

Sometimes when he had friends over, I could see by their body language that Ilyas was bothering them. Or that by their tone of voice that they are warning him to ease up. He doesn't pick up on these cues.

Ilyas and a friend are playing video games on the couch. He gets up to move something and when he sits back down, he sits too close to his friend. His friend scoots over and so does Ilyas. They continue to play but Ilyas yells too loud and laughs too hard. His friend has no more room on the couch. Ilyas has crowded him into a corner. So I take him aside and explain how his friend may be feeling, hoping to make him more socially aware.

Like empathy, learning social cues, can be taught. Kids that don't have these skills because of past traumas or abuse, need help learning how to interpret these cues.

People watching can be invaluable for that. I would take Ilyas to the mall and as we sat and ate ice cream, we watched crowds of people go by. Groups of teenagers, moms or dads with their children, couples holding hands, all streamed past. I asked Ilyas to tell me if he could guess what people were feeling based on their expressions and body language, and tone of voice. He got pretty good at it and while it was like a game to him, he did begin to get better at reading people and figuring out his role among them.

Journal Entry #22 (Summer)
Regrets

This is Ilyas' second summer with us. Ilyas has declared he doesn't want to go to any camps. He just wants to stay home, but we need the break. While he is progressing, he is still such an imposing force in our lives. He is a "larger than life" sort of person. He enters a room and he has a presence. I can't ever ignore he is here...he turns heads wherever he goes. I have been telling him, to use his power for good and not for evil. He has power - it is just innate.

Zak had volleyball nationals in Atlanta the end of June. I gave Ilyas the option to go with us. Biff, Zak and I were all going and would be gone a little over a week. I thought it would be fun for him to fly out and stay in a hotel with us. He hadn't behaved well at the last few tournaments, complaining constantly, but because we were going to be gone for so long, I wanted to give him the choice. He chose to go to a camp instead. He thought the trip didn't sound like much fun. His YMCA camp began at the same time and I enrolled him in another camp for the extra days we would be gone.

As we got closer to leaving, I could tell he might have regretted his decision, however I kept assuring him of the plans. It wasn't like him to be worried, or at least let us know he was worried, about being away from home.

Dropping him off at camp went well. The staff was happy to see him. There was a day between camps and because Sue, our usual go-to caregiver was also gone, another respite worker picked him up. She took him to her house and planned to take him to the second camp the next day. That night he used her phone to call me in Atlanta. With the time change, he woke me up at one in the morning. He was really upset and wanted to come out to Atlanta to be with us. I stayed on the phone with him for over an hour and assured him we would be home in a couple of days. He couldn't be consoled and continued to call four or five more times that night. He missed us and cried. He never slept that night. I realized then he had truly and deeply bonded with us. I knew he loved us, but this was different. This was an emotional plea that was unexpected and heartbreaking.

He did go to the camp, but he didn't do well. The camp called and wanted him gone. Sue, back by then, picked him up and kept him until we got home. Ilyas knew if Sue had him, he would be okay and get back to us. I think that while he missed us, his feelings of being abandoned reared up again, and he still wasn't sure we would come back, or want him back. He continues to fear that we won't be there for him, as he knows we don't plan to keep him permanently. He knows because he still asks us to adopt him.

This was a different feeling from the kid who had kept me at arm's length most of the time. I knew he loved us and wanted to be part of our family, but he had never asked, or begged for that confirmation. That made my heart tender, and when we finally got home, he flew into my arms with genuine love and affection. He stayed close for several days after, becoming my shadow again. I knew we would have to address this deep attachment sometime soon.

The rest of the summer flew by. We were able to use his funding for volleyball camp and a local sport camp that runs all day for a week. We bought him an Arcade Pass so he could go as often as he wanted. These activities have had an amazing effect on him. All the life lessons that go along with being on teams and learning new skills, are invaluable. He has to listen, focus and perform. He is meeting kids outside of his small elementary school. This is huge for him. He can't carry the stigma of being a foster kid if they don't know he is a foster kid.

As it turns out, Ilyas is a sponge when it comes to sports. He follows directions well. He mimics and copies his coaches when it comes to learning the fundamentals of the sport. He has amazing footwork and movement. He believes all these coaches and that makes it fun for both of them. Now if we could only get him to believe his teachers and family...

How, as foster parents, can we compartmentalize our feelings and emotions for the kids we care for? I taught school for years, coached for years. My kids' friends came in and out of our house for over two decades. I was fond of all of them, loved many, and grew especially attached to a few, but I could always separate my life from theirs. Probably because they had their own lives.

Foster kids don't have their own lives. They are completely dependent on others for their basic needs. All are orphaned in a sense, and all of them are vulnerable. Vulnerable, fragile, broken children coming into your home. That can't help but bring out a tenderness in a parent.

"Foster parents need to protect themselves from getting too attached." We are taught that in training. But protecting ourselves does the child no good. Attachment is what these kids need. These children come into our lives for days, weeks, months or years, and then they leave. We have no idea when that might be.

We begin by trying to hold our foster children with stiff arms, at a distance. But then our arms soften, weaken, then dissolve into love, affection and compassion. How can they not? After all, isn't that what all foster parents really sign up for? To love and care for abandoned or troubled children? Attachment unfortunately comes with the job. There is no compartmentalizing the feelings we have for these kids.

I knew I had to go into foster parenting with both feet, eyes wide open and a welcoming heart. What I didn't realize is how this is not just a job. It is not just a commitment. Foster parenting is a surrender of emotions, a battle of consciousness and a relinquishing of all preexisting ideals.

Journal Entry #23 (Fall, 2 years)
Puppy Love

Ilyas is in 4th grade! He was put into a 4th/5th combination class which will be good for him. He will be challenged academically and socially with older kids. I requested a conference with his teacher right away. We talked for a couple of hours. "All About Ilyas".

I thought maybe by disclosing his past and present situation, I could help her to help him. I knew he had a reputation that precedes him. It was a great meeting and I left feeling confident in her as a teacher, and a mentor. I wasn't wrong. She held him to a high standard and brought out the best in him. She discovered his "hidden talent" of writing. Hmmm, all that writing I made him do was not wasted! She understands how he operates and while she is compassionate, she is not a pushover. She holds him responsible for himself but is in his corner when he needs assurance.

Partly due to maturity, partly due to increased self-confidence, and a lot to do with stability, Ilyas has stepped back from confrontation and is taking a breath. We haven't seen the bullying type behavior he was used to using. It could also have something to do with love.

He is in love with a 5th grader. He wrote her an endearing love letter, which he naturally didn't give her. Of course, she is not in love with him, a lowly 4th grader, but that doesn't seem to matter much. He realizes he doesn't have a chance with her. I am impressed that he is handling this so well. He can talk about it and doesn't get agitated. In fact, he talks about it every day. "Mom, she is the prettiest and most popular girl in the whole school." "Mom, she told me she liked my essay and my shoes today!"

I know all about "his crush." I taught her and her sisters in preschool. He chose well. She is truly the nicest of girls and very sensitive to others' feelings. She would never say a mean word or be judgmental, which I am so thankful for. Ilyas' triggers to his worst behaviors are rejection and abandonment.

Zak has left for college. Ilyas is missing and calls him often. We let him move into Zak's old room, and that has helped. They became so close over the summer, I was afraid Zak's moving out would cause him to melt down. But the new drug free Ilyas, is showing compassion and understanding. He misses him, but he also knows it is important for Zak to go to college and he is trying to support that.

> Good times with my brother 2009
>
> When I moved in Zak's room I relized it wasn't worth Zak's leaving. Zak's room was full of memories and his stuff. With Zak gone, I really understand now that you don't know what you've got till its gone. But I have memories that no one can take away.

We seem to be in a good place right now, skating through each day with minimal upsets. Am I picking my battles or is it real? Ilyas is opening up more about issues instead of fighting internally with them. He is eager to talk it out which leads to a better ending overall. He wants to process or discuss his feelings with us. That is a new, and somewhat exhausting, behavior. We are having longer and more productive conversations about being responsible for and owning behaviors.

I told him that all kids go through many of the same issues he faces day to day. That what he is going through is called "ages and stages," and every kid goes through these stages. It's normal. He is always surprised when I tell him that other kids deal with similar feelings and problems. In one way, I reassure him he is normal, and in another way, I am taking away his idea that life is not "All About Ilyas."

Foster parents, like all parents, need to be advocates for their children. While advocacy may feel normal for a biological parent, it can sometimes feel forced or insincere for a foster parent. Much of the time, foster parents don't feel a deep connection with the child, especially at the beginning. Advocacy takes time, commitment and persistence. Parents must feel compelled to fight for the good of the child.

Two top issues worth fighting for are the health and education for the children in your care. In fact, as a foster parent, you are mandated by the state to provide adequate care for your child, in health and education. However, providing adequate care can sometimes mean requesting services that are not easy to get.

When Ilyas came to us, he had a mouth full of rotten teeth. Quite a few were missing, and those that remained were rotted or capped in silver. One of the first appointments we made was for the dentist. Foster kids are on MediCal, and it was my first experience with that system. The only provider in our area proved to be a large dental franchise.

We went to the first appointment, sat in the waiting room for over two hours, and then went back to a curtained cubicle among ten more cubicles. The dentist was going between four or five patients at a time. I appreciated the dedication from the staff to offer services for low income or foster families, but, for a kid with ADHD, this was not the best situation. He was scared of the dentist already. His teeth hurt all the time, and this wasn't the right atmosphere for a personal relationship to form.

I spoke with our family dentist whom we had gone to for many years. He agreed to bill Ilyas under MediCal, even though he was his only MediCal patient. This offer came from his heart. He treated Ilyas kindly and like a part of our family. He pulled all his rotted teeth and even came in the office on a holiday when Ilyas was having a toothache.

I found that finding doctors willing to work with us and accept MediCal wasn't that unusual. Often doctors, by the pure nature of their desire to help people, would make an exception even when they didn't routinely accept MediCal insurance. Our own family doctor who didn't have any MediCal patients, saw him several times for free. Our orthodontist offered to provide braces for Ilyas pro bono. Again, a gift from the heart. Braces aren't an option and are not covered for foster kids on MediCal.

It took time, effort, and some coaxing or arguing my cause, but being an advocate for his health care paid off. He formed personal relationships with many of his physicians, all of whom made him feel significant and worthy. And it made him feel *normal*.

"Only 50% of foster kids will receive a high school diploma.

Only 10% of former foster youth will attend college and, of that 10%, only 3% will graduate. That means only 0.3% of former foster youth will graduate from college."

Advocating for education takes dedication and a personal interest in your child. Parents must stand up for the right of every child to get the same quality and quantity of education that the rest of the class is getting. Unfortunately, this isn't always a given with foster children, or any child with special needs.

To be an education advocate might mean asking for your child to have extra time to take tests, or to take tests in a quiet room. It could mean requesting a child sit at the front - or the back- of a classroom. It might mean explaining to the teacher the reason your child is behind in class; it may be due to the many placements and schools they have attended. Not because they aren't bright. It could be that you need to ask for meetings to talk about your child feeling lost and alone on the playground, feeling victimized for simply not living with their parents. Advocating for your children's educational rights can mean so many things.

By meeting with Ilyas' teacher early in the school year, I hoped to avoid the same kind of burnout reaction that happened his previous year. I know he can push buttons and exhaust those that are trying to help him. I have been battling that myself for two years now. I felt that understanding what his triggers are, and his methods of dealing with them, can help a teacher get and keep the upper hand.

And again, I found that most of the time the teachers, principals and counselors want to best help each child. Teachers teach because of their love for children and the desire to help them learn. They often don't know what is going on unless you tell them, and in all or most cases you know your child better than anyone.

If a child has an IEP or a 504 (education plans), foster parents must be involved in these meetings. Often foster parents "hold the educational rights" for their children. This means they have to sign off on any education plans put in place by the district, and therefore have a huge impact a great deal of input. It is up to us to make sure the rights to the same education as their peers is upheld.

Bearing in mind that only 50% of foster or former foster youth will graduate high school and 0.3% will graduate college, this is where foster parents must make an impact. We need to make sure that education is a priority to these kids and that we encourage, no, implore them, to stay in school and keep graduating!

Journal Entry #24 (Late Fall)
Anticipation

Halloween and Thanksgiving have come and gone. Ilyas dressed up in Billy's old football uniform for Halloween and attended a party at the home of a classmate. When I picked him up, the father told me how nice and well-mannered Ilyas was. Whhaaatt?? Well, good for him. I am happy he can behave in a socially acceptable manner away from home, then let down his guard and lose it at home sometimes. That is normal!

Thanksgiving was a nice family holiday this year. That is the one holiday our family makes sure we all are together. More important for us than Christmas. Ilyas knew he had the power to make or break the holiday. We have a lot of family and they are all close. He did great! Is he maturing? Is he feeling more secure and safe? Is the tough love paying off? I guess it's a combination of everything.

Ilyas continues to do well in school. He is writing and reading a lot, and playing baseball, basketball, and volleyball. He joined a local club volleyball team and at nine years old, is the youngest player on his under 14's team. The team travels all over the Bay Area playing tournaments and he is having a blast.

While Zak has left for college, Zoe has come back home for a few months after her college graduation. Ilyas loves Zoe! He thinks she is perfect. He tries hard not to disappoint her. She is more critical of his acting out behavior than Zak was, and more critical of the discipline that follows. He thinks she is beautiful and is awed by her athleticism. In return, she is always in his corner when he complains about friend issues and playground spats. She always has supported the underdog and is helping Ilyas see that he can hold his own without reacting. That helps all of us. She helps him with homework and he does chores around the house more willingly when she is home.

Another birthday for Ilyas! He is ten years old. These birthdays feel different, than those of our other kids. For him, each trip around the sun is a big deal and nothing is taken for granted. We had a family birthday party with a few family friends. I am not setting him up for a failed friend party, again.

We've decided to take Ilyas with us to Costa Rica for Christmas. I am excited, but also a little apprehensive. This is a big deal for him. He's never been on a family vacation before. We haven't been able to trust his behavior and we were always trying to avoid meltdowns and reduce stress and tensions, but he deserves this. He's worked hard this year to control his temper and calm down his behavior. His struggles and efforts have not gone unnotice

And now, just like that, it has all switched. Ilyas is dark and moody. He won't speak unless he is saying something mean. He doesn't like anything; food, outings, movies; nothing. Being uncooperative and testing limits is the new normal. He wants to pick fights and argue. It is hard not get drawn in and then it escalates. I have been sending him to his room in the evenings and telling him I'll see him in the morning. For both of us it is important to totally disengage.

Is this him trying to sabotage his upcoming trip? Is he thinking we will back out and leave him home? He may think just get it over with, and he won't be disappointed, because he knew we wouldn't take him anyway. He is wrong. Come hell or high water he is going on this trip and he is going to enjoy it!

Self-sabotaging behavior happens when an action creates problems and interferes with long-standing goals. When a child does something that changes their goals, the first thing we need to look at is what's going on underneath this act? Much of the time there's some sort of fear. Fear of failure, fear of success, fear of rejection, or fear of embarrassment. Most often, it is a fear of feeling unworthy.

"We are our own worst enemy" rings true for most of us. Unfortunately, even when we can connect a behavior to self-defeating consequences, there is no guarantee that a person will disengage from the behavior.

Springing this huge trip on Ilyas, though excited to go, must have felt overwhelming. He probably didn't feel he was up to the test. He knew he had failed family get-togethers before with his behaviors. I couldn't allow his self-sabotaging behaviors to get the best of him, or me. While I had to address the attitude, I understood the underlying cause. We had to convince him he would fit in, be fine, and have a great time. He needed to be convinced he deserved to go as much as anybody else.

I wonder now how much pressure that put on him. Knowing he had to be on his best behavior, and fitting into a family vacation that required a passport. He had to handle the many changes that come with traveling; plane transfers, different food, climate, and culture. Our kids grew up taking long road trips and vacations out of the country. Ilyas had never even been on a plane before!

Foster kids generally have low self-esteem, low self-worth. While it might look counterproductive, and frustrating to us, for foster kids, sabotaging good things is a form of self-protection. Sabotaging behavior results from a misguided attempt to rescue themselves from their own negative feelings.

As parents, we must continually point out the good things that have happened or worked out well for them. Kids need to get in the mindset of thinking about what has gone right, as opposed to what has gone wrong. We must try to change the default setting in their experiences. Change it to a positive.

Foster children will often focus on the negative, which continues the self-sabotaging behavior. As children get older they tend to sabotage themselves by using drugs and alcohol (self-medicating) or cutting (self-injury). They impede their own progress, so it is imperative that foster parents notice this behavior and work to correct it early.

This again goes back to self-worth, esteem or respect. Although exhausting to keep up a damaged child's confidence, it is crucial for these kids to realize they are worthy. Not only to realize it, but to believe it and trust it. Only when they feel deserving can they appreciate their future and what lies in store for them.

Journal Entry #25 (Winter)
Family Time

Costa Rica! What a trip. Since we'd been there before and stayed at the same place, this trip felt smoother. There is nothing better than having all five kids together for the holidays, and to be away from the stresses that come with work and school.

Zak and Ilyas have been inseparable. This is the first time they have really spent time together since Zak left for college. Ilyas learned to surf and he ate all the food the rest of us did. I felt most of the time he worked hard to not lose his cool.

He did have a few meltdowns, and I seemed to be constantly explaining that this is the way families do things when they are on vacation, and this is a family vacation. He has no experience with family vacations and the dynamics that play out.

Having said that, this IS a family vacation. A time for rest and relaxation. For me as well as the rest of the family. Catering to a ten-year old's mood swings is not relaxing. Often, I felt like we were walking on eggshells around him, waiting for the next incident that would set him off. On the whole though, he was a trooper, especially on the way home.

Zak came down with a bad ear infection along with an infected cyst in his ear. The long flight home was especially painful for him. Ilyas sat next to him the whole way home and never slept. He made sure Zak was comfortable and nothing bumped him. I had never seen him take care of anyone before and I felt very proud of him.

Ilyas had never been on a family vacation before. With <u>any</u> family. Imagine trying to fit in with a group that has grown up together and hoping to become a part of them. On one hand, Ilyas was desperate to make us like him and etch himself deeper into our family. On the other hand, he had no idea how to handle travel, unfamiliar food, different language, and the family dynamics. To top it off he was still dealing with a quick temper, meltdowns, lashing out verbally and mood swings.

While Ilyas was excited to go, I hadn't considered how traveling would thrust him into his hyper-vigilant mode. He was constantly on the lookout for danger and abandonment, not trusting that we had everything under control. He was afraid he and we would get lost or attacked.

Vacations are meant to be relaxing. Especially for children. As parents, we still have the responsibility of caring for our kids, but Ilyas was still distrustful of our care of him. He seemed stressed and barely slept on the plane ride over, even though we flew through the night. We had a six-hour drive from the airport to the house we were renting. We drove through the jungle and the mountains, and still he didn't sleep. He was keeping watch.

It wasn't until we got to our house and he realized he and Zak were sharing a bedroom, did he begin to relax. He explored the area, and quickly memorized the path to the beach, the way to the store and around the yard. Finally, he relaxed his control on the situation, became calm and swam, surfed and read. The joy of seeing the wonder in his eyes when he rode horseback through the jungle or saw the monkeys in the trees at our house was worth the trip alone.

Luckily, we had ten days to spend in Costa Rica and by the end of it, he was a different kid. He understood he was included because we wanted him there, and trusted that Biff and I would watch over him, not leave him or let anything or anyone harm him.

Journal Entry #26 (Spring, 2 ½ years)
Recess

Ilyas complains every day that he has no friends, and no one wants to play with him. I try to explain that friendships go both ways. He needs to play what they are playing, do what they are doing. I told him to try to walk up to a group and just join in. Be compliant. He tells me he tries, but everyone runs away from him, leaving him alone.

He is not getting in trouble at recess this year. He hasn't been suspended once. But he is sad, dejected. I finally told him to go hang out in the library at recess, which he is doing, but I know he desperately wants to engage with friends.

Ilyas was blamed for something that happened on the playground, which he couldn't have done. He was in with his teacher at the time. The boys that accused him got in trouble for lying and making up the incident. I noticed Ilyas felt a little stronger, walked a little taller for a bit. Then of course, as life plays out, he is never off the hook. A week later these same boys passed around a notebook for everyone to look at except him. More kids started laughing, pointing at him, and making faces.

Thinking it might be about him, Ilyas told the teacher who confiscated the notebook. Inside was a drawing of a monster labeled "Ilyas is weird." All around that page and the next, were derogatory remarks about Ilyas, written by the kids. The same boys were disciplined, and Ilyas was once again not the one in trouble. This made the boys even more vengeful, and they continued to taunt and tease him. Kids can be so cruel. Now, he didn't tell on them anymore, he just retreated to the library in sadness.

I felt bad that I had such low expectations of his behaviors. So low, that I thought he obviously was to blame for all issues with friends. It turns out he had been trying hard to fit in, but the kids at his school didn't want him to change. It was more fun for them to be able to taunt and tease him and watch him react and get in trouble. Once he stopped reacting, they tried even harder to get to him and finally just excluded him from playing with anyone at recess.

Every parent experiences their own heartache when their child is hurting. Ilyas was hurting inside, and it broke my heart when others teased or bullied him. He was so vulnerable and fragile. He put up this tough exterior, but it was very thin. You could scrape it away with a few words or even a look. He couldn't let people know he was suffering, so he just withdrew to "that place"; the dark, pouty, angry place where he spent so much of his time. The place inside himself where he would put up a wall and not deal with anything or anyone.

And then, there we were - his family, who continued to invade his space and demand he join us in the light, and we would love him and make it right for him.

What most upset me was that I could understand that Ilyas behaved in a way that was representative of a child that never had unconditional love. Representative of a child who had been beaten, abandoned, abused and molested by the very people who were supposed to protect him. Instead, many adults, though aware of his story, were not willing to excuse or even understand his actions. The impression I got from other parents was that Ilyas should be "fixed" by now. After all, he lived in a good home and should be thankful and appreciative.

But what are the excuses for their children? The children who are mean to him and won't include him. The same children who bully, taunt and tease him just to get him to react and get in trouble. These children seemingly come from good, intact families, and have all they want or need. These same parents want Ilyas to handle the teasing and taunting, but where is the accountability for the teasers and taunters?

Ilyas has issues he is constantly working on and trying to take responsibility for. There are reasons behind his behaviors but still we are working to change those behaviors. I think the main reason these "normal" children acted in mean and spiteful ways, comes from the "foster kid" stigma. They see Ilyas as a little less of a "real" kid and therefore, his feelings are expendable.

Journal Entry #27 (Late Spring)
Another Big Change

We have decided to change schools for Ilyas in the fall. We can see that life for him won't get easier staying where he has so many issues with peers. What started as his disruptive and aggressive behavior in second grade just couldn't be undone or forgotten. He couldn't get rid of or change his reputation.

We were lucky to have another elementary school in the district and also near our house where they could accommodate him. I would have fought for the change of schools had they not.

Ilyas' second season playing basketball was amazing! He loves everything to do with the game. He played for the same great coach and it was the bright spot of his week. Ever since we put that ball in his hands a year ago, he has developed a passion for the game. It's great to see him have a passion for something.

In Little League he moved up to minors where the kids pitch, making games longer and less engaging. He wanted to pitch, catch, or play 1st base, but mostly played outfield where the game was a little less stimulating. He might only get one ball per game hit out to him. He did run all the way from left field to right field on a couple of occasions, to beat the other fielder to the ball, but was reminded to stay in his own spot. Even though he had a good season, he isn't sure he wants to play baseball again.

(Summer)

Ilyas finished fourth grade achieving good grades and high test scores. He is showing signs of how bright he is. Now that he is off all meds, and settling in to the structure of school, he is more willing to follow directions and cooperate in his schoolwork. I often tell him to "show what you know." I am trying to convince him that teachers want to see what you have learned and the progress you have made throughout the school year.

He is excited to move to a different school for fifth grade yet feels sad he is leaving the first stable school experience of his life.

We decided not to send Ilyas to any sponsored "foster kid" camps this summer. He doesn't want to go to camps for foster kids and wants time to practice being a normal kid. He did go to the YMCA camp, by his choice. The leader asked him specifically to come. He had a blast swimming and playing basketball on the new courts. They just built new dorms in the redwoods that resemble tree houses. This was the first time that a camp director didn't call us mid-week to report bad conduct!

He flew by himself to visit the older siblings in San Diego. While he stayed with Bekah and Ryan, they enrolled him in surf camp and water sports. Ryan took him to play basketball at the local Rec Center. At Billy's, he went to the fair and to watch the Chargers football team practice. It was a pretty special trip and he felt so important flying by himself.

The rest of the summer went well for the most part. He hung out a lot with Zak, who was home from college. He went to a local daily sports camp at the high school as well as volleyball and basketball camps. This required a fair amount of driving him to and from, but it was worth it to see him happy and healthy.

He continues to progress in his daily behavior as well, trying extra hard to maintain a good attitude and keeping his temper in check.

He persists in asking us to adopt him. "Please, mom!" he begs. "I'm trying really hard to be good and I won't be any trouble, I promise."

We knew we would have to answer him with more than the usual, "It's not you, we aren't planning to adopt anyone."

So we sat him down and we told him that as long as he kept progressing and working on his behavior, he could stay with us. We told him he had a place at our home for as long as he wanted. We didn't mention adoption and we didn't elaborate, and it seemed enough.

For now.

Foster kids want permanency. Let me rephrase that; ALL kids want permanency. All kids deserve permanency. A place where they can set down roots, where there is unconditional love and unfailing support. All kids thrive under those conditions. They yearn for that place they can call home.

Children want a home where they can believe people will love them when they are bad, as well as good. A "forever home." Families provide us with our sense of who we are, where we belong, and how we are connected.

Ilyas was taken from and returned to his birth mother five times. CPS (Child Protective Services), offered her parenting classes, put support systems in place for her to go to counseling and to drug rehabilitation. She continually failed to show up or complete the requested tasks and eventually stopped her visitations to Ilyas.

There are two major roles for CPS. The first is child protection and the second is establishing permanence for children. Their first commitment is to help the birth family keep and care for the child. CPS is responsible for the entire family, not just the child.

Shortly after a child is removed from a home, the county which has jurisdiction holds a hearing, where a judge decides whether the child's safety requires they be removed and placed in the temporary custody of the courts. In California, approximately two weeks from that initial hearing, the courts determine if allegations of abuse and neglect against the parents are true. At that time the courts decide whether the child fits one of the descriptions in the Welfare and Institutions Code, which authorizes the courts to intervene on behalf of the child.

If the court declares the child is a court dependent, then they have to consider who should care for the child. Often this is a relative. If placement with a relative is not possible, the child is placed in a foster home.

In most cases, including Ilyas', the court orders a reunification plan, so the child can return home. The plan describes the responsibilities for the parent to fix the problems that caused the child's removal in the first place.

The courts must review the cases of all children placed in foster or relative care at least once every six months. There, information is given on the parent's progress with reunification plan and how the child is doing in foster care. The court may return the child to his parents or he may remain in foster care.

A permanency hearing must happen within twelve months of the date the child entered foster care. At this hearing they must decide whether the child can return home, stay in foster care and/or if efforts to reunify should end. Ending reunification services does not terminate parental rights. The parents occasionally continue to have visitation with the child even when reunification has failed.

For Ilyas, his mother was found to be non-compliant and he therefore became a ward of the state. Which made him now adoptable. This is how he came to be at several fost-adopt homes. These were homes ready and willing to adopt a child; apparently just not Ilyas.

We saw that Ilyas desperately wanted us, our family, to be that forever home for him.

Asking us to adopt him, was heart wrenching for us. We realized we could adopt him, as he was "adoptable" by the courts. The problem was, we weren't ready and willing to become adoptive parents. We had signed up to be foster parents. We hoped by assuring him he could stay with us as long as he wanted, he might feel that was enough.

Even making that promise to him was hard to do. We were committing to raising him for another eight years. Then he would be eighteen, old enough to "age out" of the system.

Selfishly, I sometimes thought about life without foster parenting. With all four kids now in or graduated from college, our lives would be our own. We would be parenting adult children only, and free to travel or relax.

But then I would look at Ilyas and my heart would soften, and I couldn't imagine my life without him. I didn't want to lose him. At the time, giving Ilyas the assurance he could live with us for as long as he wanted, was all I could promise.

Journal Entry #28 (Fall/ Winter, Year 3)
Fifth Grade

Ilyas is in the 5th grade at his new school! This is his fourth school year with us and he has the most amazing teacher this year. He has his first male teacher, with a ton of experience and a fantastic reputation.

There is no after school YMCA, but it is connected to the middle and high school where I coach. He stays after school each day and hangs with me or plays on the playground until I'm done coaching. So far so good.

The year started well. Right away he fell in love with several of the girls and they with him, "the new kid." The boys group was harder to break into. These boys and their parents have been friends for years. They've had their play dates and social lives set up for a long time. While the group is nice, there is no real inclusion into the inner circle - common phenomenon in small communities. I think back and hope I was never like that as a mom with our other four children. I don't think so....I've never had the time or energy it takes to maintain those kinds of inner circle relationships.

His reputation somewhat preceded him (in our small community), but he was determined to make a good impression. Thus, began a new behavior of wanting to impress people by trying too hard and doing anything for attention or appreciation. This meant being too helpful, too happy, too funny, too loud. We are trying to tone that down. I explain that people will like you for who you are. He doesn't believe me. That hasn't been his experience so far. But, he hasn't let very many people see who he really is. Certainly, he has never had the confidence to let his peers see the real Ilyas. That Ilyas is kind, generous, thoughtful but vulnerable.

At conferences in November, his teacher pegged him as a leader. He says that Ilyas shows great leadership skills. Awesome! A guy who leads others has to be feeling pretty good about himself and confident in his abilities.

Fifth grade curriculum. The class had a unit on the "Route To My Roots." He had to write an essay and present it orally. There was also the "Timeline Of My Life" and his paper on "Family History." Never before had I realized how painful these kinds of assignments can be. There are a lot of kids out there that either don't know or don't want to acknowledge where they came from. Especially at age ten. They just want to be accepted, to fit in. So they make up a pretend life, a fantasy life, but everyone else knows the truth all along.

Ilyas wrote his family history story about being a Martin. In the end it set him up for teasing. The other kids knew he wasn't really a Martin. He is not Irish. He doesn't have the same skin color or facial features. They made fun of him and called him a liar. We made a mistake letting him hand that writing in. But what do you reveal about a child whose history is unbearable and unbelievable and not appropriate for other ten-year olds to hear?

For the next project, his timeline, we worked together and helped him navigate between what he should divulge and what he shouldn't. In his mind, his timeline started when he came to us, at age seven. But the assignment was from birth. He wrote that he was born in L.A. He didn't have photos, so he drew a picture of himself in a crib eating out of a Nesquick container.

Then a picture of a kid with no teeth. Then shelters and group homes. He didn't have a family. Toward the end of his timeline he crammed in photos of him from age seven to ten. Sports pictures, pictures of his dogs and cats, and pictures of our house and family. This was real. No one teased him this time.

School continued to be positive for Ilyas and he was having more good days than bad days. His teacher worked out an agreement with him. When Ilyas felt frustrated or edgy, he could take a book from the class library and sit in the back of the room and read. If he was disruptive or disagreeable, his teacher would send him outside the door with a book. His teacher showed Ilyas amazing understanding and compassion. Rather than reacting to him, he understood Ilyas needed a break from the situation and offered that. He didn't engage nor humiliate him. Soon, Ilyas could monitor himself better and spent less time outside but always knew it was an option.

The mother of one of the girls that had a crush on Ilyas, volunteered occasionally in the classroom. She decided she didn't want her daughter associating with him. The girl told Ilyas this and he told me. I told him to back off his friendship with her. I explained that this sort of puppy love relationship is quick to come and go and to move on to a new one. He agreed, because there was another girl on his radar already!

Apparently, the little girl wasn't as eager to let it go. She was used to hiding things from her over-protective mom and wanted to continue to be his "girlfriend" in secret.

The class went on a field trip to an Imax, and the mother of the girl and Zoe both were chaperoning. Zoe knew nothing of this romance and Ilyas was already flirting with a new love interest. When they arrived at the theatre, this girl wedged her way in to sit next to Ilyas.

Her mom was a row or so away, but when she saw the seating arrangement, she stood up and told her daughter to move. Rebelliously, her daughter wouldn't budge. Mom insisted. Daughter resisted.

Then the mother got personal. From a row away, she shouted to her daughter, "You are not allowed to sit next to Ilyas. He is trouble, a bad kid, and you cannot be friends with him."

Zoe stood up and said, "Excuse me. That's my brother. And you shouldn't talk to kids that way."

Zoe made the girl move seats. Ilyas was embarrassed, humiliated and hurt. Zoe did her best to cheer him up, but words hurt. Especially adult words. His confidence crumbled.

A couple of weeks later the mom called me at home. She was still worried that Ilyas and her daughter were secretly "dating." These kids were only ten years old! I told her Ilyas was already "seeing" another girl and wasn't interested in continuing a relationship with her daughter. She beat around the bush for a bit and then came out and said that because Ilyas was a foster kid, she was concerned that he would someday bring a gun or a knife to school and hurt someone, namely her daughter.

I assured her he would never do that and ended the conversation quickly. I was shaking, I was so upset. She was accusing Ilyas of terrible things with no basis of truth behind it. Only because he was a foster kid.

Ilyas heard about all this at school. The little girl told everyone what her mom thought and said, and now I had to field questions about his mental health and stability to the community. All based on one person's unproven and hypothetical suspicions. Her opinions were based solely on the fact that he was a foster kid.

He had to live down a new reputation that he was violent and unpredictable. He had to try to repair irreparable damage to his self-worth.

How often does this happen to kids? Foster kids. Again, judged solely on the fact that their parents didn't or couldn't parent them. That in itself does not make a kid bad.

THE FINAL REPORT AND FINDINGS OF THE SAFE SCHOOL INITIATIVE: IMPLICATIONS FOR THE PREVENTION OF SCHOOL ATTACKS.

By the United States Secret Service and United States Department of Education

Although much blame is associated with "broken" or dysfunctional families, the US Secret Service discovered that most school shooters come from two-parent families.

• Almost two-thirds of the attackers came from two-parent families (63 percent, n=26), living either with both biological parents (44 percent, n=18) or with one biological parent and one stepparent (19 percent, n=8). • Some lived with one biological parent (19 percent, n=8) or split time between two biological parents (2 percent, n=1). • Very few lived with a foster parent or legal guardian (5 percent, n=2).

I felt bad for Ilyas. He'd been doing well socially at his new school. Now he was faced with proving himself innocent of a crime he would never commit.

As for the curriculum, it was eye opening for me to see how some assignments are so hard on different kids. Talking about their past is often something a child has bottled up or internalized for several reasons. One could be the ridicule and embarrassment because of being poor, abused or neglected. Another reason could be plain old pain. Talking or acknowledging a weakness is painful, especially at the hand of a parent.

Ilyas did a great job, turning his pain into reality. By explaining that he had Nesquick for meals, he wasn't comparing himself to a peer having pancakes. It was just his reality, without apology and without shame. Talking about it helped and he sought neither pity nor sadness. It was his life and sharing it was cathartic.

Today, educators are more aware of the diversity in the classroom, but we have a long way to go. Though as a society we used to ignore differences, we now acknowledge them but often still don't talk about them. Every child in every classroom has a story. We must remember to try to find out the parts of every child's story that make them who they are.

When I coached, I often took a day to ask each player to share something about themselves that no one else on the team would know. It was eye opening, not only for myself but for the rest of the team. Now we could look at each player and see someone that has a past, is dealing with the present, and whose future is still being built, and molded. Often by us.

Journal Entry #29 (Early Spring-11 years old)
Trauma and Trust

Ilyas,
It has been three and a half years since you came to our home as our foster son. What a time it's been! I can only describe it as a journey, a trek, an adventure, an experience. We are happy we have been able to care for you. You are very special. Our job as parents has been to love, nurture and teach you. I'm sorry we couldn't always protect you. I love you,
Mom

Social services asked us to take in another foster boy (13 years old). He didn't have anywhere else to go. We were told that, like Ilyas, he loved basketball and sports, and perhaps our family would be a good influence on him. We weren't told much else.

We enrolled him in the local junior high and from what I could tell, he seemed to fit right in. He and Ilyas played basketball together in the afternoons and video games in the evenings. He went home to see his family on weekends. After a couple of weeks, Ilyas began to complain that this kid was bothering him. Taking his stuff and trying to get him to break the rules. Soon he was complaining about everything about him. He stopped playing with him and hanging out with him. But that was Ilyas' MO. Complaining. I chalked it up to the fact he missed getting all the attention .... It's always been "All About Ilyas" and now he had to share. Share his room, his toys, his games, family, everything.

One day after school, when I just had Ilyas in the car, he told me he needed to tell me something. While asking him what was on his mind, I felt distracted and impatient. I thought it was complaining...again. He hemmed and hawed and coughed nervously. I gave him time to sort through his thoughts, but it wasn't like him to choose his words carefully. Usually he was bursting to talk. Then he told me that he was really scared of the new foster brother, and that he had tried to get him to do bad things. I wondered what could scare him? What was this new boy doing that could make Ilyas so nervous, timid and frightened?

It was our house, our rules, our family. That hadn't changed. He told me then that every night his new foster brother was coming up to his top bunk and trying to molest him. So far, Ilyas had warded off his attempts as best he could, but this boy had succeeded in getting into Ilyas' personal space and each night was getting worse. He had manipulated Ilyas into thinking he had no choice in the matter. They were both foster kids. No one would believe Ilyas anyway.

At first, I wondered if Ilyas was making it up. Those were strong accusations and would surely bring the hammer down on the new kid. I had him tell me it in a different way, asking abstract questions. He stuck to his story all the way. I asked him to call his sister Bekah (previously a social worker) and tell her. She talked to him, then told me to remove the kid, asap. Ilyas was telling the truth.

I called the county and reported the incident. They said they would try to work out a solution in the next day or two. What??? I wanted the kid gone, now. Ilyas wasn't safe in the house with him another night. Biff was on duty at the firehouse, so I asked Sue to take Ilyas until we could remove the other boy. I went to bed that night feeling nervous and frightened. I felt it unwise to confront the boy myself. At thirteen, he was big, angry, manipulative, and I was alone.

The next afternoon the social workers came, confronted him with the accusations, and after initially denying it, he confessed. It happened just like Ilyas said it did.

If there ever were a time when I longed to hold and comfort Ilyas, it was then. He was still at Sue's house, protected and safe. I felt guilty and sad that I didn't listen more closely and carefully to his complaints.

We had a meeting at the county office regarding the incident with Ilyas and the new foster son. The social workers wanted us to agree to keep him, at least until a new placement could be found. They brought in his primary caregiver and she disclosed the issues she had with him that led to him being in foster care. According to her, he had molested his siblings and cousins. She said that she had to lock the siblings in their room at night, so he couldn't get in. She had neglected to tell the social workers these details when they took him into custody. She loved him but did not want him back.

CPS was originally called in by his school district for allegations against him for molesting or harassing kids at school and in the neighborhood. That led to him being put in foster care. The mother didn't dispute the allegations. We were never told about the reason he was placed in foster care.

Why wasn't this caught before? Why was it not divulged to us? I never would have agreed to the placement. I never would have intentionally put Ilyas in harm's way.

Going through this whole ordeal was especially hard on on Ilyas. Conjuring up old memories and bringing to the surface the pain and hurt from his past experiences of molestation was hard for him to bear.

The emotional and physical damage could have been much worse. At age eleven, Ilyas was once again subjected to someone forcing their will on him, putting him in a victim's unwilling role. This created intense conflict for Ilyas. He told me later he decided to take the upper hand this time. He wanted to control his destiny. So, he took a risk and confided in me.

Trust. Ilyas trusted us to help him. For that, he had to believe we would listen to him and that we would understand. And even more, that we would take measures to help him.

This was the first time he fully trusted us. Earlier, he would have thought that he was on his own. Either he had to act alone or accept that this was his fate. All because he was a foster kid and had to look out for himself by himself.

Needless to say, we did not agree to keep the placement for the other boy. Ilyas was our main concern and we needed to keep him safe. He needed to feel safe, loved and protected.

Ilyas was slated to be "downgraded" from the ITFC (Intensive Treatment Foster Care) to a normal status. Which would have been great news for him! He wouldn't be considered in the hardest or worse cases among foster kids anymore. However, because of this experience, his social worker felt it important he continue to be offered services for therapy and counseling. So, he continued to keep his higher level of care.

My Mom takes me to tournements and practices. She supports whatever I do. She makes good food. She likes the Beatles.

My Mom is very creative. She loves rearranging our house. Its been changed like 35 times. She also has great vision. She also arranges our yard plenty of times.

My Mom is smart. She does math really well. She is good at memorizing things. The only math she can't do is Geometry.

My mom is really chill. All I have to do is ask before I do something, and she says yes. She never embarrases me in front of my friends. They love her tator tot surprise.

She's a good cook. She has plenty of different recipes. She learned it from my grandma.. She is my Mom.

Journal Entry #30 (Late Spring)
Sports

With sports being such a big part of Ilyas' life, sports related issues were bound to pop up. Sure enough, poor sportsmanship reared its ugly head. While athletics in general have been amazing for him, the nature of sports themselves draw competition, and someone has to come out on top.

All the hard work that Ilyas put into practicing and going to camps to work on skills and drills has paid off. He is pretty good at everything and the best at some things!

He wants to be the best at everything. This seems to me, a normal growing experience for a lot of kids. The difference here is that Ilyas doesn't have the tools or coping skills to handle losing or being second best. Disappointment is still a huge trigger for him. If he doesn't score a lot, or doesn't win, he has a hard time controlling his disappointment. And disappointment turns into anger and resentment.

Fifth grade recess is as important to Ilyas as the classroom. Games are fought and either won or lost here. Pecking order is established. Life lessons are abundant. Group mentality runs rampant. Recess is where integrity becomes valued and empathy is rewarded, or brute force becomes king and hard work, determination, and strength beats all.

We are working to instill in Ilyas a respect for the game. To handle competition with respect and dignity. The lesson is long and hard. We tell him if he wants to play competitively, he has to be able to handle all aspects of the game. We do not want to raise a poor sport. He already has social issues and we don't want to add to them.

He is learning the give and take that happens between pre-adolescent boys. What a delicate balance it is between being a bully or being a victim.

Ilyas either has to learn to handle hurt feelings to avoid feeling vulnerable or play a victim's role. Or if he's on top, then he feels he won't get picked on, but being on top can mean others will turn on you.

He is figuring out how to navigate his way through these complicated dynamics.

Unfortunately, he continues to operate much of his time in survival mode, where it is "look out for yourself" regardless of the consequences.

The end of fifth grade came fast. Ilyas finished with good grades and won several awards. The one he is most proud of is his President's Physical Fitness Award. Next year - middle school. I hope they're ready!

All About Ilyas

"**Zak is fun, cool and creative. He loves hiking. He's tall with black hair and skinny legs. He's strong, with a face that's easy to remember. His voice is deep and wise with a hint of sarcasm. He plays volleyball. He is a middle with considerable power. He knocked out a kid and broke another kid's jaw with a volleyball." By Ilyas**

When our kids were very young, I told them a story about building a "character house." I asked them to think about how we build with Lincoln Logs. You start with a good strong base or foundation. Then you build up from there.

To build a character house, the kids would add a log every time they did something well or made a good choice. It takes a long time to finish this house. It takes an entire childhood! If there are bad decisions or choices made, then you have to take away a log. I prompted them by reminding them about adding a log now and then for a job well done. Granted these houses existed only in their minds, but a child has a vivid imagination and our kids were always aware of them.

My mom used to use the same concept with us. Only she would say, "You've earned another jewel in your crown." Her crown related to heaven, and when we died we hoped to have an enormous glittering crown, heavy with diamonds, stones and jewels. I took her seriously, and always thought in the back of my mind I was sorely lacking in the precious gem department. Even as an adult I felt proud when she told me something I had done earned me a jewel in my crown. Whew! I may make it yet.

Kids don't need tangible rewards when they make a good choice or a great decision. They don't need ice cream, candy or a prize. They need a mental or visual support they can build or take apart in their minds as they grow and learn. They won't always succeed, and they will fail. Children need to know their character won't crumble because of one failure or even two. And they won't be done building after one or two successes.

I talked to Ilyas about the character house. But he thinks in black and white. Most foster children do. It's either good or bad, right or wrong. It was hard for him to visualize his own house.

So, we talked about other people. I made up a random person, gave them a name and related a story close to something Ilyas had done. We discussed it, pondered it, analyzed it, and as long as it was someone else, he could pass judgment. And he often did, harshly. My hope was that he'd apply the lesson to his own life. Based on his choices lately, he has. He doesn't realize it, but his character house is coming right along. Strong and sturdy.

Journal Entry #31 (Summer)
Agreement Between Mother and Son

Summer is here, and our lives are full of volleyball and basketball tournaments, practices and sports camps. Biff and Ilyas have been going fishing some afternoons and we visit the bookstores and libraries every week. Ilyas has been working at our preschool summer camps with Zak and the kids love him. We have made several small trips and it is good to see Ilyas healthy and thriving. And growing! He has sprouted up and grown three inches in just four months.

On the flip side, it is so easy to get drawn into Ilyas' often demanding behavior. I find myself engaging in battles that can't be won or lost. They just are long drawn out arguments about something he wants (immediately), or something he wants to do. Either it is inappropriate, untimely or not in my power to give. Yet it still becomes an issue that goes on for hours! Often ending in hurt feelings, pouting, and both of us saying things we don't really mean.

Ilyas will grasp at anything to get his way or his point across. If he is really mad at me, he will threaten to leave. He tells me he will find foster parents that understand him. He is bluffing and quickly realizes it. Then he backs down and mumbles under his breath. He doesn't want to leave, and it is an empty threat. But he is eleven.

I, on the other hand, am not eleven and know better than to stoop to his level. But I sometimes resorted to threats also. I threatened to send him back if he didn't change his behavior. I told him if he really wanted to stay with us, he wouldn't do so many things to get in trouble. That wasn't fair of me, and I felt bad as soon as I said it.

I can't imagine how that felt to him, after promising he could stay with us as long as he wanted.

Parents should never intimidate a child with threats of abandoning them because of their behavior. Ugh! I would never have used that threat with our biological children. Because it wasn't an option. But both Ilyas and I knew that, as a foster child, it is an option.

Frustrated by Ilyas when he would push and push, and I often felt at the end of my rope. I resorted to push back with comments I knew would not only stop the behavior but also hurt him and make him feel vulnerable. That is bullying. Not one of my finer parenting moments, and I'm ashamed to admit it.

When any parent (foster or not) bullies their child, there are lifelong side effects. Most foster kids have experienced bullying from their bio parents, social workers, siblings, teachers and peers.

When bullying parents use this style of parenting, they try and motivate their children by being derisive. This can be especially damaging, since it can encourage a child to think they are worthless. This can leave mental scars that can result in depression, as well as set the child up to have difficulty sustaining good relationships. If a child learns how to treat people from the example of a bullying parent, he or she is likely to grow to be a bully as well and may have a hard time developing healthy relationships.

So Ilyas and I made an agreement. It was the most emotional agreement I've ever made and both of us were in tears. I agreed I would never threaten (because it was just a threat), to send him back, and he would never threaten (because it was just a threat), to leave. Ever again. We never did.

Journal Entry #32 Fall - 6th Grade
Pick Your Battles

It feels like the days are rapidly turning into weeks and the weeks into months. Life with Ilyas is becoming normal for us. The new normal. This is the beginning of his fourth year with us! We love watching him play sports, get good grades, write amazing essays and make friends.

He tried out for and made the sixth-grade basketball team. Quite an accomplishment since over one hundred kids tried out and only fifteen were selected. Ilyas has a great sixth grade core teacher and changes classrooms for English, Science, Math and P.E. It's hard to believe he is in middle school now.

The days run together, and for the most part, the good outweighs the bad.

However....I sometimes forget what the day to day can be really like. Because time is passing so quickly, I don't want to forget what really happens day to day.

A week with Ilyas-

Monday- Good day at school. After school he had basketball practice, then home for homework, shower (which he hates, but sixth grade boys smell), dinner and bed.

Tuesday- Ilyas received after-school detention for teasing and taunting a classmate. He was just one of several boys involved. They teased; the kid reacted, and a fight ensued. Ilyas wasn't involved in the fight, but he was there and was part of the group that initiated the confrontation.

We talked about it when he got home. We discussed disengaging from the "crowd," or walking away. Or better yet, urge them to leave the kid alone, that it was a bad idea. We reminded him of how he felt when teased and bullied. He didn't have much to say except to first deny he had any part in it. Really? Then he tried to justify it. This same kid had teased Ilyas when he was in second and third grade. The usual lecture followed - two wrongs don't make a right, be the bigger person, take the high road, be a leader. Pretty much a one-sided conversation.

<u>Wednesday</u>- Ilyas invited five boys to come home after school before their basketball game. The plan was to hang out here, eat an early dinner and then go play their school basketball game. The boys were playing outside when I received a call that they were caught climbing on the roof of the church behind our house. They were all being held by someone working at the church. I went and brought them back and told them to stay on the property. Again - pack mentality/bad choices.

Ilyas was furious because it wasn't his idea and he felt the boys disrespected him and his house by getting in trouble. But who was also on the roof of the church? Ilyas.

I fed them and packed them up for their game. The team they played was inexperienced and Ilyas, who was used to playing a lot, sat on the bench while other kids from his team played. He was very angry after the game, complaining that the worst player on the team got to play more than he did. Plain poor sportsmanship and behavior we don't tolerate. Now we had to
also talk about that. He needed to be a team player and support everyone on the team. He had a really hard time coming out of his dark mood.

<u>Thursday</u>- After Ilyas went to bed last night, we discovered he had created a "Twitter" account and reactivated a Facebook and email accounts. He has been in trouble twice already for this. Obviously, the discipline we have used hasn't been effective. We told him he wasn't allowed to have these accounts until he was thirteen, complying with the rules set up by the companies. He agreed to our rules, even signing a contract stating he understood. The contract has since disappeared.

We took away his phone and i-pod for a month and the month was up a couple of days ago. We gave him back his phone and he re-upped his accounts immediately, knowing he wasn't allowed. We had to address this Thursday evening. At first, he lied and said he didn't do it. "Honest, Mom!" We had proof of course. His Facebook page listed him as nineteen and from Montana. His twitter name was derogatory. He showed little or no remorse so now he can't have any privileges. He abuses even the smallest amount of freedom.

Biff put on a password only he knew and programmed Ilyas' ipod so he could only listen to music, but not use any other features. He can't use the computer except for schoolwork with a parent or sibling monitoring him. He can't stay home by himself and has to go on even the quickest errands with me. Ilyas was defiant throughout. He claims of course, that everyone else gets to have these accounts and we are not fair.

Later, when he felt less defensive and open to discussion, I explained to him we would provide him with everything he needs. Love, family, shelter, and because we cared about him we would go to any length to keep him safe and secure. The rules we set down were there to protect him.

He keeps busy with sports and we added even more structure to his schedule, meaning he is even busier now with little down time. It is what he needs right now to stay focused and out of trouble. He hasn't been making the best decisions, so he needs to step back and reflect on his choices.

So that was last week! I tend to forget the stresses of each week as soon as it goes by, but this is a fairly typical week...just change the behaviors.

The week was just that; a week of "All About Ilyas" as every week is. The big picture however, is positive, not negative. Yes, it can be exhausting to parent this child. But this to me, is normal twelve-year-old behavior! How many other families in the country had the same battles last week with their pre-teens?

First, the issue with group or pack mentality. Wanting to belong with a group sometimes leads to bad decisions. Choices are made in exchange for camaraderie and feeling included. Ilyas needs to find his own voice and not let others dictate what he does, especially when he knows it is wrong.

I am encouraged by the fact he was upset and felt disrespected when his friends didn't follow the rules while at our house. That shows me he has pride in his home, property, and rules. It affected him when others didn't honor that and felt different to him than things that happen at school.

Poor sportsmanship is an issue I think we will be working on for a long time. Perhaps forever! He is passionate about his sports and with passion comes a sense of righteousness and dedication. Also comes fervor, excitement, rage, and a zeal for the task at hand. Passionate people get things done. They make a difference in the world. Maturity will help temper his intensity, but I never want him to lose his passion for the game or anything else in life. Being passionate however, is no excuse for being rude, angry or sullen. And certainly, to project those feelings is not going to get him anywhere. Again, "use your power for good, not evil" comes into play.

Social media is another pre-teen infatuation. Not being forthcoming and honest however is the bigger issue. Dealing with the issue of integrity is big. A life lesson and another life-long lesson. Sneaking, or being deceitful to get what you want is obviously the wrong way to go about it. Yet, at the same time, I think parents often set their kids up for this scheming behavior because of the strictness and restrictions they put in place. It is like the forbidden fruit. If you deny access to the Internet you are only delaying the process, because a child will quickly find a way around it, with or without your knowledge.

Like it or not, I would rather my kids are up to date with technology. In this situation, education is the key. Trying to set passwords and blocks are not going to last long when the child is smarter than the parent and much quicker. By restricting Ilyas, we basically set him up to sneak his way onto the computer, or when the restriction was lifted, he immediately opened and went to sites that were not allowed. This time around I took away the privilege of getting on the computer by himself, but I began asking him to help me with computer related issues, Facebook posts, purchasing online etc. By working with me, I had his rapt attention and he felt important. I used the time to talk about risks and rewards of the different aspects of being "online." As my trust in him grew, and his belief that I trusted him grew, he became open to a more truthful dialogue. We could chat about issues and because he didn't feel defensive, he would share stories with me about tales he'd heard about the Internet as well. He also quickly proved that he could do far more than I could, faster than I could, understood more than I did and became a big help. In a couple of months, we let him get a Facebook page, which by then had lost a lot of its appeal. He learned a lot by learning the hard way, and it opened doors for him in regard to trust and honesty.

Though it sounds again like big issues, and they are, they are common issues. We rejoice in common issues. Those we can deal with! What is new is the fact that his abandonment and neglect issues haven't had as much of an impact on his behavior as in the first years he was with us. His past abuse and trauma isn't playing a part in his choices. He is being twelve. Thank goodness.

Excerpt from an essay - by Ilyas (6th grade - age 12)

I think it is a good idea to write about me because I have a great story. Sort of a rags to riches story. My children and I will look back on this and see the darkness that spread on my life before the light. The amount of pain that was thrown upon me should be shared. People should know there are worse things in life than death itself.

When I first moved here I was a ticking time bomb, angry and wanting to beat down everything I saw without thinking of the consequences. I've improved a lot. My brothers and sisters look like angels. They act absolutely perfect and it kinda bugs me sometimes, but then again, my family is kinda perfect. Except during holidays when we fight and yell. It makes me laugh cause it's hilarious what they fight about. It has to be about food or who is the favorite child. It's me obviously.

Journal Entry # 33 Winter - 6th Grade
A Victim

Ilyas has been nominated by his teacher, Mr. O., to attend a leadership conference in Washington D.C. If he goes, he will represent his school and district. We are so proud of him! It is a great opportunity and we are determined to make it work out.

We've been talking about tattling. About not doing it! For a while now he's been telling me everything that happens at school or with friends and it is draining and tiring. There is a lot of information that goes into a day in the life of Ilyas, told me, by him, mostly in the form of complaining. I appreciate that he is open with me, but tattling is not a quality that will win you a lot of points with peers.

So Ilyas stopped tattling. He must have thought he simply needed to internalize those feelings instead of expressing them. Sometimes that is the right thing to do, but I wonder if he thought I just didn't care. So quietly, and over time, he became a victim. He allowed kids to tease him, and he didn't react. He stopped getting in trouble. He stopped talking about conflicted issues that arose at school.

Then one day I got a call from a concerned teacher. A week earlier, there had been a disruption in the classroom. A boy had been bothering Ilyas for days, making fun of him, taking his pencils, blocking his path and the like. One day, the boy teased and taunted Ilyas all class and Ilyas ignored him. Then the kid knocked Ilyas' pen off his desk. When Ilyas stood up to retrieve it, the boy bumped into him and pushed him over. This time, Ilyas yelled at him, grabbed him and pushed him back. The boy caught Ilyas in a chokehold and held on. Ilyas was literally being choked, lips turning blue, gasping for air, when the teacher intervened. The boy was suspended. Ilyas was allowed to stay in the classroom, and never said a word about it to me. Neither did the school.

A week after this incident (which I still knew nothing about), the boy's father came to school in the morning to drop off his son. He walked up the side stairs and found Ilyas. This dad confronted him, *grabbed his arm and started to yell at him. He told Ilyas he was a bad kid and to stay away from his son. He called Ilyas a "fag" and told him he would hunt him down wherever he went. The father threatened he had friends that were cops and said something about finding Ilyas' dad (I'm sure he didn't know Biff was a burly six foot five). Other kids witnessed this and ran to the office. The administration made the dad leave with a warning never to come on school grounds again. This is when his teacher called me because he was concerned for Ilyas. He said Ilyas seemed depressed in class.*

The subject of adoption has come up again. Though we assured Ilyas he can stay as long as he wants, that sounds like a halfhearted promise, even to me. We've made sure to take away his power of making adult decisions because we want him to be a child. Yet it sounds like a choice we are offering him "as long as he wants" when he has no choice. If he did, he would choose to be adopted. By us.

How is it that whenever Ilyas did ANYTHING wrong, we were called right away? He had been suspended once and served several detentions this year over minor offenses. Never fighting, cheating or hurting someone. He'd been called in (as we had), over accusations of him defacing the walls in the bathroom. Proven innocent - not even at school that day. Called in (as were we) over kids bullying and accusing Ilyas of perpetrating the incidents. Again, proven innocent by witnesses. He was constantly called in to the office. Because of his newfound victim role of not tattling, or reacting, he was the perfect scapegoat. In the case of the chokehold, he was actually hurt! The teacher confirmed Ilyas was not at fault, but we were never called.

This time, Biff and I were upset. Receiving a heads up call by his teacher that Ilyas seemed despondent in class was a red flag that no one can overlook. He is still considered an "at risk" child because of his diagnosis of RAD and Depression. There needs to be extra care taken to monitor this kind of child because of the increased rate of self-harm or suicide.

We drove to the middle school office and talked with them. They brought in Ilyas. The assistant principal explained they intended to call but hadn't had the time. Hmmm, time was never an issue when he was the one they called about. Biff told Ilyas the father was wrong for doing what he did. That it was illegal for him to come on school grounds and touch a child. Ilyas was aghast! He asked why no one had helped him, if that were true? He told us he was terrified that the man was a child molester and would find him. In his twelve-year-old reality, he was convinced he was a goner.

This father had been out of line before. His son was constantly in trouble and the parents were blaming everyone else. This time it was Ilyas. With a known history of confrontation from the parent, the school should have even been quicker to act in support of Ilyas. They should have called him in to make sure he was okay after the dad confronted him. They should have told him themselves that the school does not allow parents to threaten or touch children. They knew of the incident but didn't take the time to include Ilyas in the equation.

His biggest fear is still being taken away from us. When he is suspended or put on detention it holds more consequences for him than other kids. It must be reported to Social Services, his social workers, and his therapist. How much more damaging is that to an already fragile child? A child that believes he is bad, confirmed by others he is bad, is a child that needs extra support. Instead, he got the opposite.

In this incident, Ilyas needed the same school that blamed him for so much, to step up and make sure he didn't feel blamed and shamed in this situation. But they didn't follow through. They let him slip through the cracks by not recognizing that he needed to hear he was a good kid and sometimes things were not his fault. He needed to feel protected by the school and assured it was a safe place.

This school is a good school. The administration and staff are excellent. How did Ilyas fall through the cracks? I don't want to believe that his feelings and well-being are a little less important because he is a foster kid. I fight that feeling because I believe in this school and in these people. But the "writings on the wall." They are engaged and concerned when Ilyas does something wrong, but when he is the victim and they could help him, they didn't. He hurts like any other child. He is more terrified of his future and of his actions than most. He is vulnerable. The administration needs to remember that foster kids have a heightened sense of awareness as to how they are treated and perceived than "normal kids" are. They are surviving.

Ilyas continues to see the world in black and white and when I told him enough of the complaining and telling on his friends, he took it literally. Which to him meant to stop communicating about what goes on at all.

We had to explain to Ilyas that while we didn't want to encourage tattling, he did need to stand up for himself when he felt bullied or teased. How do you do that? It takes confidence and inner strength. He has more of that now. He just needed to hear it was okay to make the distinction himself. He had to choose to not be victimized, and not so sensitive to others that he reacts and then they pounce. Surviving in the pre-teen world takes fortitude and patience. Surviving in the pre-teen world as a foster youth also takes courage, spunk and perseverance.

Journal Entry #33 Spring - 6th Grade
Love and Leadership

Ilyas asked a seventh grader to "go out" with him. A big and bold move, considering he was a sixth grader and she was "The-Most-Popular-Girl-In-School." She agreed to be his girlfriend, and the relationship lasted a typical middle school two weeks. He was devastated when it ended. It led however, to some beautiful love poetry or at least break up poetry...

Excerpt from a writing entry on "The One" Ilyas, age 12

She makes my heart beat like OT in game 7 of the finals. She is as beautiful as the evening sunset, smart as Einstein. She has everyone looking. The way she smiles makes your knees weak.

The truth is, I'm still in love with her. She's always in my head. I'd change anything for her. I'd quit basketball and volleyball. I'd do her homework. Anything!

She flashed by quicker than an all-star basketball game. I'm sorry for whatever I've done. She is the end to all my troubles. I miss her!

Ilyas decided on his own to try a new therapist. Though mandated to continue therapy, he was cleared to take a break for a few months. He wasn't cooperating with the therapist he had, and she was frustrated with his lack of progress. He felt comfortable with and respected his psychiatrist but had never truly connected to a therapist. He came back from his first session and couldn't wait to return. They discussed his friend issues, girls and school. He confided in her. He disclosed and revealed issues that he needed to get off his chest. It was a great fit for him and she knew how to get him to open up. This is a huge breakthrough for him. What a relief! She was local, knew our family, and had a lot of experience with teens.

Ilyas is also experiencing another form of bullying - racial insults that are unacceptable and disrespectful. And of course, the usual, and no more acceptable, foster kid slights. He has been told that his parents worked in a rice paddy - he told them he has never been to China. He was teased that he can't see well because his eyes are slanted. He replied he wears contacts. Told that he doesn't belong here because he is brown. He told them he sits out in the sun a lot. Kids have told him his parents didn't want him, that he is temporary, that he will be a criminal, and that he is unloved.

He has met these taunts and disrespect with far more integrity than I thought possible for his age. He replied to the kids with a simple explanation. He's been neither rude nor defensive. His responses caused the conversation to end instead of escalating. I am cheered by this very huge change in him in just a short time! He is listening to us and his therapist. Yay!

It makes me sad to think of all he has to endure. Our other kids were never teased or bullied like this. He has so much material for kids to use against him, just because of who he is and how he got here. All we can do is instill in him the knowledge that he is special, he is loved and he is good. I think he believes it or at least considers that we believe it!

There is so much written on bullying. There is a ton of advice available on how to handle it, how to advocate against it, and how to avoid it. Until your own child is a victim of bullying however, all the information isn't relative or relatable.

I am, and have always taught, against bullying behavior. I have seen it in my classroom and more often on my sports teams. Coaches intimidate, teammates torment, parents of teammates heckle, referees harass. On the playground there is bullying. In the classroom there is bullying. I regularly advocated for a bully-free class or team, but it happens still, all around you, all the time.

Two things have to happen to setup a bullying environment. First, you have the bully or oppressor. They take power or pleasure from antagonizing someone else. That behavior can stem from an insecurity. Or a belief that they are better than everyone else. They feel better about themselves when they can make others feel weak or uncertain. Whatever the root to their behavior, their action will go nowhere unless they can find an audience or victim.

That is the second part of the equation - the victim or casualty from the attack. I believe if we can teach our youth to avoid being a target or even better, how to handle the taunting or teasing, then the bully has no hold or power. When Ilyas countered the taunts with calm comments or humor, he avoided feeling powerless and at the same time shut down the beast.

Self-deprecating humor can be used with huge success in a lot of these circumstances. Making fun or taking jabs at yourself, wards off anyone else being able to needle you.

Ilyas is getting better at this. He told a kid who teased him about being Asian, "Well, I'm not good at math so there goes that stereotype!"

All the kids laughed and that was the end of that. If a person can make fun of their shortcomings and flaws, then no one else has power over them to use their weaknesses against them. But being Asian isn't a shortcoming, weakness or flaw.

Yet Ilyas was caught between someone wanting him to react and himself wanting to tell the kid, you're an idiot!

If Ilyas were to defend himself and say he was proud to be part Asian, it would have given the other kid an advantage to keep pursuing the subject. Ilyas, without renouncing his ethnicity, left with the upper hand.

Another way to avoid being a victim is to ignore, avoid, or walk away. Sometimes that works, sometimes it is impossible. Bullies take that as a weakness and it bolsters their self-importance. They, in turn, will intensify their dialogue or body language. Confrontation is out of the question. Most bullies pick on kids smaller and quieter than themselves, counting on an easy target. Fighting back is no longer allowed or accepted.

My advice to parents is to educate themselves and their children on what bullying is and how to stand up against it. Each child has their own personality and each child has a limit as to how much they can take. Talk about it. Often. Everyone is capable of bullying behavior and everyone is capable of victim behavior. It is important to not succumb to either. Arm children with confidence and courage. Teach them to be an advocate for themselves and others. Growing up is hard and kids can be cruel, but they will grow up. We want to create young adults who have learned to be compassionate, self-assured, hopeful and composed.

Besides being the victim, what about the bystanders that watch, say nothing or worse video the bullying and post it to social media? Kids want to fit in. They don't want be the one who rocks the boat no matter how they feel about the situation at the time. A bystander, by definition, is a person that knows what is happening, yet stays silent and doesn't get involved. We urged Ilyas once again to use his power for good. Use his leadership to get involved and speak up. He must have taken it to heart because with just a couple of weeks of school left, I heard from a teacher at his school that Ilyas stood up for another child that was being picked on. The principal of his middle school wrote us a note telling us that Ilyas intervened in a fight between two boys. He stopped the fight when everyone else was standing around watching. He is making progress in so many ways and I'm confident his future will be full of extraordinary stories.

An email from a teacher whose son had been the victim of the assault -

"I meant to email you sooner, but it's been kind of a zoo here. I'm sure you've heard, but my son was attacked by another student. Several students jumped in and tried to break it up; my son didn't fight back because he was afraid he'd get in trouble. One of the things he remembered from that scary scene was "S" swinging through the bars in the pavilion, grabbing my son and turning him so he absorbed the blows not my son. And then "S" walked him up to the office. It was a pretty powerful moment. I told "S" that and that I was proud of him. But most importantly, I told him thanks for watching out for my boy."

Journal Entry #35 (Late Spring -6th grade)
Loss

Ilyas' great grandfather passed away this month. We broke the news to him as gently as we could, but he was pretty broken up. It's more than just an older relative dying. He lived off and on with his great grandparents throughout his life and they were the only link to his biological family. Though he hadn't seen them as much the last couple of years, they were nearby and a tangible connection to his past. We encouraged Ilyas to talk about the good things he remembered, and the lessons he learned from his "Tikun." We all learned from Tikun. He was a distinguished man who valued honor above all else. Though he couldn't raise Ilyas himself, he had a strong belief that our family was put in their lives for a reason. He felt Ilyas was safe and his future was secure with our family.

At the funeral, Ilyas got up on his own and stood in front of the crowd to talk about what his Tikun meant to him. Besides the minister and planned speakers, Ilyas was the only person to get up and talk. We cried. It was a moving speech and a brave thing for a twelve-year-old to do.

His great grandmother, Tipau, gave Ilyas a gold pen that had belonged to his Tikun. He treasures that pen! She moved back to Hong Kong soon after to be with relatives and now Ilyas is here, with us, as his only family.

We were able to swing Ilyas' trip to Washington D.C. for the World Leadership Forum. We put in request forms through social services, to be signed by a judge, so he would be allowed to go. There were costs involved and we requested and received funds for his trip through social services. It is a pretty awesome thing to be nominated in general, but for a foster child, it is unheard of. He was nominated based on merit, leadership and academics. Biff flew there and back with him, but he spent the week with his group. A group of kids from all over the world.

He represented his school, our school district, the county and the State of California. He had to take off a week of school to attend. The trip to Washington D.C. was a growing and maturing experience for him. Ilyas visited all the usual D.C. sights, and also had the opportunity to sit in on the House and Senate. He participated in mock debates and voting. We received great feedback from his advisors. They commented he led several discussion groups and was the best lobbyist they'd seen. We already knew that! We've started calling him Senator.

All About Ilyas

Ilyas signed up for Track and Field and has done quite well. He is the last leg of the relay team and runs in several other events. This keeps him busy, and along with basketball and volleyball he is active, tired and content.

The rest of the school year quickly flew by. We had thought about enrolling him in the smaller charter school on campus for next year, but he has ended the school year strong and confident.

He received his last report card - straight A's! Wow. I remember his first report card...straight U's (unsatisfactory).

P	COURSE	Q4	Ab	T	Ct	Comments
1	LA 6	A-	0	0	S	Pleasure to have in class
2	6th Technology	A	2	0	O	Wonderful to have in class!
3	PE 6	A	0	0		
4	Science 6	A-	2	0	S	
5	Math 6	A-	0	0	O	Positive attitude/cooperative
6	Soc. Stud. 6	A	2	0		

4th Quarter Grade Point Average = 4.00

Bekah and Ryan are getting married this summer and have asked Ilyas, along with Zak and Billy to be in their wedding! He is thrilled. But a little unsure. Everyone else is an adult. He wonders why they would want a twelve-year-old kid as a groomsman. We have to order him pants, a shirt and a tie that match the rest of the boys.

The trip to Washington DC meant much more than just attending a leadership conference. No one there knew Ilyas was a foster child. His sixth-grade teacher nominated him based on leadership qualities and academics. He was there on his own merits and I felt it should stay that way.

I think that's why it was so important to me that we follow through to make sure he could go. He was in a group of fifth through eighth graders and kids were there from all over the world. They had discussions on global issue topics including world peace. World Peace! This was a child that five years ago couldn't find peace anywhere in his life and now he was involved with and leading discussions on it. Maybe that is what makes this experience so valuable. Ilyas has seen the bad parts of growing up, experienced the worst that life can throw at a child. He has learned how to get things done. How to accomplish something. How it feels to long for something and do whatever it takes to obtain it.

With all the red tape and bureaucracy that social services is, it was enlightening to know that if you ask for something you just might get it. We were not only able to get permission for Ilyas to miss school to attend the conference, we were able to allocate funds for his trip.

Sometimes it feels like foster kids are part of this huge network and they get tossed around, then spit out. Much needs to be fixed with this system. But this time they came through. Ilyas has amazing social workers. His main worker has been with him throughout his time in her county. She could have let him go, or shuffled him to another worker when his case became burdened with records and reports. She didn't. She stuck with him because she truly cared about him. She was instrumental in getting him services when he needed them. And shutting down services when he didn't need them anymore. She made sure he got a passport when we took him to Costa Rica. Those particulars require a good deal of time, reports and follow up. Maybe they shouldn't, but they do. She hung in there with Ilyas when he was disrespectful and rude to her. He didn't want to be a foster kid. He didn't want a social worker.

To help Ilyas understand the system and how he fit into it, we started taking him to his court dates. He had a court date every six months to update his file and make sure he was on track. Often there are changes for foster kids every six months or even sooner. He was not mandated to attend, but I felt he should know what goes on and who is making decisions about his life and his future.

The same juvenile court judge presided over all cases in the foster care system. Once he started attending his court dates, the judge would ask him to sit up along the bench when his case was heard. He was petrified at first, but she asked him questions about his activities, his sports and his grades. She took an interest in him. She put him at ease and though he was merely a case number to most, he felt he was significant to his social worker and the judge. He was able to talk about his improvements and that helped push him to keep progressing.

Ilyas also had a social worker from the local agency. She consistently went out of her way to help make things happen for him. He hated the weekly meet-ups so instead she tried to catch his games and sporting events when she could instead. He was never nasty but clearly never warm and fuzzy toward her. Yet she persisted in trying to get to know him and work around his and my schedules.

I mention this because I also met with social workers that were inept, uncompromising and seemingly unfeeling. There were rude standoffs and rigid rules. Working within this system is a look at opposites. The foster system is put in place to help kids that don't have parents or caregivers able to care for them. Yet the process and procedures involved with finding and maintaining care for these children sometimes makes it hard to believe they were there to help.

As with any agency, there are levels of staff and every level has a job. There are intake decisions, medical needs to determine, then finding a home, maintaining a placement and all the while working toward a permanent solution. For each child. Often there are sibling groups and the social worker must work for the whole family, including the parents not just the children. So that involves reunification sometimes against the better judgment of the foster parent or people on the outside looking in. There is so much to consider for each and every case that it is overwhelming the people that work the hardest - the case workers - burnout and turnover are the costs they pay.

We were lucky to have social workers that became social workers because of their desire to help children. Regardless of the low pay, long hours and putting up with every kind of parent imaginable; most are devoted to making life better for a child.

It is important that foster parents understand they can advocate and receive funds and assistance from the county or state. I believe the more activities a foster child is involved in, the quicker he realizes his worth and the expectation that he is valued. Many times, it is cost prohibitive for parents to sign their child up for sports, camps or clubs. Yet there are ways to obtain help through scholarships and grants. It is time consuming, but so necessary and so worth it.

I was frustrated many times with what could have been a simple request for something that would benefit Ilyas, only to be bogged down in paperwork, meetings and lengthy waits. There is no streamline process and while that has its benefits, it also means kids aren't able to take advantage of programs and activities that could help make them feel like a regular child. Which, if asked, all foster children want to be.

Journal Entry # 35 (Summer)
What Do We Do Now?

We have had Ilyas with us for five years. I think back to the little guy who first came to us, scared and untrusting. He had no boundaries, no roots and no self-esteem. He was reeling from being tossed around in a system that regularly spit him back out when he failed another placement. No one hung on to him for long. He had been abused, beaten, neglected, abandoned and molested.

Yet he survived! He did more than survive. He thrived. He took all his disadvantages and turned them around. He learned from his mistakes. He learned from others' mistakes. He slowly, yet consistently, improved himself. He attached himself to us, learned to trust us and slowly began to repair his life.

I've realized I can't imagine my life without him. I don't want to lose him back into the system, which is always a possibility. As foster parents, we don't have much say as to future decisions. He is a ward of the state. Even though we've had him for five years, there is always a chance they could decide he would fit better somewhere else, or less cost to the state if he were in a group home.

I don't want someone else to have him. I want him. I love him. I love him with a depth I can't find words for. I love him for who he was, who he is and who he will become. He was wounded when we found him. By caring for him we gave him a chance to heal, to mend some of the damage and pain that were his life for his first seven years.

Biff and I called a family meeting with all of the kids, except Ilyas. We sat down to discuss the future. Ilyas' life with us has become so intertwined that we need to figure out as a family where this is going. Remembering we signed up five years ago to be foster parents just isn't enough anymore.

We went to a family reunion in Colorado. While there, we managed to get away with the other kids to talk and find the answer to the question, "What should we do now?"

<u>Adopt him was the answer</u>. Unequivocally and unanimously decided. Yet there were pending questions. It's a life changing decision for all of us.

1. What if adolescence and puberty bring out new or destructive behaviors?

We were agreed that if and when that happened we would deal with it then. I personally felt that I knew Ilyas inside and out. He had bared his soul so many times, nothing was left I hadn't seen. Plus we've already raised four teenagers...

2. Four now makes five. What does that do to this tight sibling group?

Agreed that four made five a long time ago.

3. If adopted, he would become legally ours in regards to insurance, health coverage and inheritance.

Not a problem. It's clear there is nothing to inherit anyway (haha).

4. We are old enough to be his grandparents. What if something happened to us?

Again, all the siblings have always had a pact in this regard. They will take care of each other. Including Ilyas.

5. What if mental issues pop up out of nowhere?

The kids felt that could happen to any one of them, at any time.

And so it was decided. We were going to adopt Ilyas! We thought about when and how to tell him. But Bekah had already thought of a plan. She and Ryan felt the time to tell Ilyas would be at their wedding. In front of family and friends.

Journal Entry #37 (August - Five Years with Ilyas)
The Announcement

"Wedding Day" for Bekah and Ryan. It was a perfect summer day and Bekah looked beautiful. All the kids were in the wedding party, and as parents, Biff and I were awestruck and proud by their sibling bond and poise.

After the ceremony and toasts, and when everyone was finishing up dinner, Biff took the microphone and asked the family to come up front. Standing together, in front of one-hundred and thirty family and friends, were Billy, Bekah and Ryan, Zoe and Beto, Zak, Ilyas and me.

Biff started talking about the little boy that came to us all those years ago. How he began and how he changed. And changed all of us along with him. Without warning, Biff was in tears. He had to stop and compose himself several times before he could continue. He mentioned that people would often say to him, "Ilyas is so lucky to have you in his life." How, for a long time, he thought about those words. "Today," he said, "I am here to tell everyone that we are the lucky ones. We are the ones that have the honor of having Ilyas be a part of our family. Ilyas, we want to adopt you."

Afterwards we were given a video from someone's phone commemorating the event. I've watched it over and over. I noticed Ilyas was nervous in the beginning when Biff was talking about him. He told me later he thought he was in trouble for having his shirt untucked during the ceremony. Then I watched as he notices Biff's emotion. Ilyas had never seen him cry. And finally, I watch as he understands what Biff is saying, what he means, and he crumples back into Ryan's arms. Then cheers go up! Whistles and applause!

We are not an overly emotional family but we all pretty much lost it on that one.

In the video, Ilyas breaks away and goes to hug Biff, then me and his siblings. Later that evening, when it was dark, and we were on the "after dinner-dinner", Ilyas found the microphone and made a heart rending speech. He thanked his family naming each person individually. Quite a boy.

Journal Entry #38 (3 years later) And, Adoption

I've always believed in divine intervention. It came from my mom who taught me that while our lives were predetermined, they can be altered through prayers to the Saints.

I believe in the "red string," or the "invisible thread." According to myth, the gods tie an invisible cord around the ankles, fingers or wrists of those that are destined to meet in life. The string may bend, twist or stretch, but can never be broken.

Destiny, fate, serendipity, happenstance, coincidence or karma, I believe in them all.

We never should have met Ilyas. Foster kids just don't cross county lines. Too much paperwork, too little follow up. We weren't looking for a child his age. Yet as soon as we met, there was a connection. When Biff first drove up to where Ilyas was staying with his great grandparents, the first words out of Ilyas' mouth were, "Dad, you're finally here!"

He told me later that he'd been watching for him, in the window for two weeks. How did he know Biff was coming? Or what kind of car he drove? According to the rules of social services, kids are not told of visits from perspective foster families.

Three years later, when the courts finalized Ilyas adoption, we had a party. A surprise party and invited his friends, our families and anyone who made a difference in his life.

Zak read a speech he had written for the occasion:

"I remember exactly where I was when I heard my little brother's voice for the first time. Ilyas was already seven years old when we had our first conversation. My parents had spoken many times about wanting to foster another kid. When I was entering my junior year in high school my mom told me we were getting a young boy. I thought *great, another kid is precisely what's missing from your life. My mom the coach, the preschool teacher, the mother to four, and the second mother to hundreds of others.*

But sure enough I was soon introduced to a charming young boy named Ilyas, or as we nicknamed him, "S".

Charming is a word I use very loosely, as it fits S for about the first two hours you know him. In the beginning we didn't get along as well as we do now. I was FINALLY getting the parental attention a last kid so often misses out on, when S stole the show. He also stole food, money, candy, and on one occasion a game boy. Once S was called into the principal's office after assaulting another student with a plastic fork. When asked what he would do differently, next time, he replied, "I would have gotten a sharper fork." At least the kid had a plan.

It most certainly wasn't all bad. I frequently found the value in having a little mini-me. I was his Kady Heron. When I wore flip-flops and cargo shorts, S wore flip-flops and cargo shorts. S is a great dancer. He was also great at taking attention away from my mediocre grades, and to this day, he is the only guy I know who will repeatedly attempt to catch water balloons falling 100 feet from the sky (to no avail).

S and I really became close when he came to visit me in college. I went out drinking with my friends and lost my dorm key. Not wanting to wake him up, I haphazardly popped off the screen and crawled through my window. I landed with a thud with the blinds tangled in my feet. I looked up to see S, scared half to death, curled up on the corner of my bed. Why would my parents let a 10-year-old visit an 18-year-old freshman at college you ask? I think the better question is why do these people keep a donkey and a goat, or why the hell haven't they gotten a pool yet?

Like I said, I remember exactly where I was when we spoke for the first time. I was visiting my siblings in my current city, San Diego, at my sister's current house, in Pacific Beach. In that exact spot, less than a week ago today, I was able to watch my little brother playing with my 15-month-old nephew. Nothing as ever seemed so natural and I knew this was the plan all along. We've been through thick and thin, to Mexico, Costa Rica and Panama and spent countless hours playing video games and volleyball. We all love you S and for the last time, welcome to our family."

I also had prepared a speech

The first day we welcomed Ilyas as our foster son, he asked, 'Will you please adopt me?' We went through tough times, countless suspensions, support counselors, therapists, calls and conversations, and still he asked, 'Will you please adopt me?' We committed to a year - as foster parents only.

It was literally the Sunday night before a Monday morning meeting that would take him away. We reconsidered our decision. We couldn't send an eight-year-old to a level fourteen group home. We were all he had.

When he was little, he was a trickster, an imposter, clever and sly. He was a shape shifter and resourceful. He was surviving. Ilyas didn't think his real self was good enough, so he had to make up new personalities and hope he would fit in. The problem was, his old self kept coming through when life got too hard, and our family knew who he really was. He thought he was fooling us but we always knew. And we liked him. Just as he was. We encouraged him to drop the facade and be vulnerable. Slowly he became who he was meant to be.

One step forward, two steps back. And still he asked, 'Will you please adopt me?' Then it was two steps forward, one step back. We put him in team sports, camps and clinics. Multiple activities going at once, tough love, hard lines drawn. We took him off meds he'd been on since we got him. He opened up, began to feel things.

Middle school came - his athletic skills became apparent. He was competitive, focused and never, ever, ever, gave up. He was determined to reinvent himself. He began to flourish, to trust, to believe in himself and his place in this world. Still the question, 'Will you please adopt me?'

When he was twelve, we told him The Big News! We wanted to adopt him. As usual in life, there were snags, delays and uncertainties. We realized to him it wasn't a done deal yet. Then he asked, 'Why haven't you adopted me yet?'

Twenty steps forward and one step back. Captain of his teams, kind words from teachers and friends, a therapist he enjoyed, A's and B's in school, a groomsman at both his sisters weddings, a devoted uncle. Finally, as of yesterday, we can officially say, 'Yes S, you are adopted!'

But you have been a part of this family since day one. You have taught us what stability and love can do. That hard work and tough love pays off. You bring out the fierce advocate in us. You repay us every day by your appreciation in the little things, the love that you have for our family, the smile that melts our hearts. You have given us all a gift. By knowing you and being a part of your life, you have made us better people. By believing in you, you were able to believe in yourself and go out and conquer your fears, weaknesses and then advocate for others.

We are so proud of you! Dad and I had to take an oath yesterday. To never betray your trust, dampen your hopes or discourage your dreams. The world is yours and we know you will do big things.

We could never have dreamed of this day without the love and support of all of you here. Every one of you has been a friend to S. Maybe you coached him and like Marguerite convinced him he was good at something. Maybe you taught him and helped him believe he was smart. Maybe you were his friend when his life was falling apart around him and stood by him. Maybe you were like Sue, Fred, Kaitlyn and Bailey who loved him and cared for him, even when he was unlovable. Or Sammi or Nik who tutored him when he didn't want to learn. Maybe you just treated him like he was worthy of a good conversation, like he wasn't 'just a foster kid.' All of you here believed in him and for that we are so appreciative and happy that you could celebrate this day with us."

S,

"S" Can't Believe 5 years have gone by
How time flies.
S I am so happy to be in your life
When your mom asked me to come out
of retirement to coach her new York
Child I was just a little hesitant
But since your mom has a special place
in my heart, I committed
And it was the Best decision,
because I Coached you !
You were my rock "S". It
was so enjoyable to watch you get better
and better each year. You brought
excitement & many points to the game.
So happy your mom
asked me to coach her son
Love
Marguerite

S —
I am so happy
for you — Congrats!
What a fantastic family
you have — A great house
full of love, laughter and fun.
You are growing up to be
a fine young man — looking
forward to seeing what the
next three years brings!
Congrats
Coach

S — one of my
favorite memories
of you is when you
had taped yourself
dancing to the
song 'Fireflies' by
owl city and your
mom walks in and
you ran to turn it
off, but you totally
got caught up. did
not hesitate to show
us that video and
thats always how I
will remember you.
Through the years
you have grown into
a wonderful person
and I can't wait to
see all the good
you will do in your
life. Its been a
pleasure getting to know
you, and whenever
let you forget about
your dope finance moves
love you S
Caitlin

S,
Well we finally got to the end
of this chapter. I know all this
social worker stuff has gotten really
old for you. and I so appreciate how
respectful you have been over the years
I have been honored to have been able
to watch from afar you grow into
a talented & smart young man
I'll always think of you when I
see Kobe Bryant or push through.
So far." You are … & the help of
your entire amazing family … make
something of yourself.

All About Ilyas

S YOU HAVE NEVER **NOT** BEEN A PART OF THIS FAM, BUT WE ARE ALL SO HAPPY THAT IT'S NOW OFFICIAL!!

WE THOUGHT OUR FAMILY WAS COMPLETE FOR A LONG TIME... THEN YOU SHOWED UP, CAUSED A LITTLE CHAOS, TURNED EVERYTHING WE KNEW UPSIDOWN AND MADE US EVEN STRONGER. WE ALL LOVE YOU SO MUCH AND ARE SO VERY PROUD OF WHAT YOU HAVE BEEN ABLE TO OVERCOME, AND THE MAN YOU ARE NOW GROWING INTO. YOU ARE OURS FOR **LIFE** NOW ☺ I HOPE YOU NEVER FEEL ALONE AGAIN. WE WILL BE HERE THROUGH THE GOOD... AND THE BAD!

LOVE YOU SO MUCH!!

RY, BEK & FLYNND

PS. YOUR NEPHEW ABSOLUTELY ADORES YOU ♥
BE NICE, BE KIND, & BE BRAVE WITH YOUR LIFE - THE WORLD IS WAITING FOR YOU!

S-

What a journey it has been! The first time we met, you had on red cowboy boots and kept sprinting across the volleyball court coaxing everyone to fall in love with you. I had only spent about 30 minutes with you and when I got on the bus to say goodbye, you cried in mom's arms. I knew from that moment that you were my brother. Yes, it is now official and it feels so good. But you have <u>always</u> been a part of this family and we would never have, and never will, let anything bad happen to you. As Zak said, there's no difference between the love of any of our siblings-- you are blood now. Ready or not, you are a Beltz for life ♡ Beto sends his love and wishes he could have been here. You have grown into such an <u>interesting</u> :) and bright young man full of potential and love. We can't wait to see what you will do in life.

Love,
Zoe y Beto

"It is great and enlightening to know you have overcome your past to find your future. Don't stop learning or loving. Grow strong and tall in yourself and don't look back.
"Keep your hand on the helm and guide yourself by the stars."

Harry
MMC8 (SW)
USN, RET.

My favorite family! Congrats on finally making the Beltz family legally complete♡ I'm so happy for you guys & I'm sorry I won't be able to celebrate with everyone. Love you guys ♡ V, Kylie

ILYAS-
I HAVE GOOD MEMORIES OF TUTORING YOU A FEW YEARS BACK. THE JOY OF MATH PROBLEMS, AND POSTERS ON NATIVE AMERICAN HUTS. CONGRATS ON OFFICIALLY BEING A BELTZ (ALTHOUGH YOU'VE BEEN A BELTZ FOR AS LONG AS I CAN REMEMBER), AND BEST OF LUCK W/ YOUR NEXT FEW YEARS, IN HIGH SCHOOL, AND BEYOND.

MR B

S-
What a pleasure for us to know you over the years and watch you grow up into such a great guy! We will always be rooting for you!
— MB

S-
I have seen you grow so much and come so far. You have truly become such an amazing, inspiring person. Don't ever forget that no matter where life takes you. Our family will always hold you close to our hearts. Congradulations on becoming a Beltz.

♡ Jasmine Jones
 & Jocelyn Jones

Although I can't make it I just want to say a big congrats to you all, especially S. I lived with my parents for 7 years before I got adopted and IT DOES FEEL DIFFERENT in that moment it becomes official! Enjoy the celebration tomorrow!

Epilogue

Hello to the readers who have embarked on this journey that my wonderful mother has written. I am Ilyas, the boy you have just read about. Surely you have questions about what the future holds for me and what I am currently doing. I hope I can answer some of them.

I am 17, close to my 18th birthday and on my way to being an adult. I'm excited for the future. I will be graduating high school in June 2018, and have applied to a plethora of colleges. I am taking my first official athletic visit to a college in Boston, with hopes of pursuing volleyball at the college level.

I wanted to personally thank you for reading this book and I hope it can change your views on fostering or adopting and give you insight into your own kid's behaviors.

I have grown up more than the words on these pages can explain.

My advice to foster parents who are having trouble with their kids is, DON'T GIVE UP. Through the darkest days for you and your child, remember that you are their only source of light and that they love you even if their words cannot express it. We are a guarded heart who know so little of happiness and light. For we have only known the dark and the cruelty of love that betrayed our loyalty.

You have given us a reason to have hope again. We do not believe ourselves to be worthy of love, for our problems greatly outweigh our benefits at first. We will grow like a rose from concrete, nurtured by you, that will allow us to grow bigger and less thorny. Praise us for even the littlest of steps for that gives us the confidence to take bigger ones. Once this step is taken in regularity, we will become the tallest rose with beauty unparalleled on this earth.

My advice to the parents who are undecided about fostering or adopting is this. Think of the relationship shared with a soul mate right now. Now imagine all that energy being poured into a child who has never experienced unconditional love. There is nothing more satisfying than watching someone grow into what you always believed they could be. Your love can change a life and will change you as a person and give you strength that you didn't know you had. It will be difficult, but the rewards are endless and will last you a lifetime.

Thank you for reading and I hope you have enjoyed this book and that you will decide to adopt or foster a child in need.

Ilyas

From Billy,

I am extremely proud of the person you have become. You have enriched all our lives in ways that are hard to put into words. I guess the best way I can put it is... it's weird to look back at the years before you were part of our family, it just feels like something is missing. You are part of the family now in every way. You have a big exciting future ahead of you, and Suzanna and I are so glad we get to be a part of it.

Love,
Billy and Suzanna

Acknowledgements

Ilyas and I would like to acknowledge all the coaches, teachers and friends that helped and supported him and our family through his early and often difficult years. Special thanks to teachers, Mrs. Anderson, Mr. G, Mr. OB, Mr. Thomas, and Mr. Morris. To tutors, Nik and Sammi, whose patience was key. His coach Gabe, who once said after a difficult, emotional game, that then he knew why he was in Ilyas' life. To help guide him. You did!

To Marguerite, Stephen, Merce, Coach C, Coach P and Papa Merce. You all made him feel worthy and strong.

Words cannot express how much Sue and her family supported us. Sue is a second mom to many, but she was more than that to us. And countless friends like the Oesterles, the Jone's, Danny, the Stratfords, Jeff F and Jeff C, and the MacLeans. And so many more, thank you!

We also want to remember that without family we wouldn't be who we are. So we acknowledge and thank our family. Our extended family that enveloped Ilyas in love, and inclusion. Especially the siblings. Zak, Zoe, Bekah and Billy. And through them, Beto, Ryan and Suzanna. They all love Ilyas with a love reserved for siblings.

I would like to acknowledge my husband Biff who supported writing this book. To my writing class that edited it, and the readers that critiqued it for me, especially Claudine, Russ, Leslie, Maureen and Cindy. A huge thank you!

I especially appreciate Katie M. for helping me get started, and to **everyone** who helped me finish. Hugs!

CPSIA information can be obtained
at www.ICGtesting.com
Printed in the USA
BVHW05s1230300718
523023BV00026B/1046/P